Creative Crowd-Breakers, Mixers, and Games

CREATIVE RESOURCES FOR YOUTH MINISTRY

Creative Crowd-Breakers, Mixers, and Games

Compiled by Wayne Rice and Mike Yaconelli

Edited by Yvette Nelson

Saint Mary's Press
Christian Brothers Publications
Winona, Minnesota

The contents of this book are reprinted with permission from *Ideas,* vols. 30, 31, 32, 35, 36, 38, 41, 43, 44, and 45, and from *Play It!* published by Youth Specialties (Grand Rapids, MI: Zondervan Publishing House).

The publishing team for this book included Robert P. Stamschror, development editor; Mary Duerson Kraemer, copy editor; Maura C. Goessling, production editor; David Piro, cover designer; pre-press, printing, and binding by the graphics division of Saint Mary's Press.

Printed in the United States of America

Printing: 10 9 8 7 6 5
Year: 2005 04 03 02 01 00
ISBN 0-88489-265-4

Contents

Introduction

Part 1: Crowd-Breakers

Part 2: Mixers

Part 3: Games

Introduction

Youth Ministry:
Its Growth and Development

For the past twenty years, Catholic youth ministry has been in the process of critically re-examining its philosophy, goals, and principles. In part, this re-examination grew out of the perceived and felt needs of young people who will be the adults of the twenty-first century. In the early seventies—before youth ministry, as we know it, existed— those who worked with young people saw a need to experiment with new styles and forms of ministry with young people. Many parishes, schools, and dioceses began to develop youth ministries on the solid foundation of relational ministry and on the unique social and developmental needs of young people. Heretofore they had relied on the unquestioned process of presenting organizational, programmatic approaches such as weekly or biweekly classes, sports programs, or rarely, weekend or overnight retreats.

The new processes and approaches planted and tended during those years produced a renewed ministry with young people based on experience and insight. Leaders in the field of youth ministry discovered that ministry with young people must be a multifaceted, comprehensive, and coordinated effort. They rediscovered the age-old truth of Jesus' ministry: all ministry is rooted in relationships. Through the leaders' outreach and relationship building, young people began to experience the warmth of an accepting community, which is vital for the development of a comprehensive youth ministry. As relationships grew, a sense of belonging and participation also grew. The experience of acceptance, belonging, and participation opened young people so that they were able to reveal the needs and the concerns that preoccupied them. Programs developed around these needs and concerns: service projects, retreats, new forms of catechesis, peer ministry, prayer groups, celebrations of the sacraments. With these rediscovered opportunities for ministry, youth ministers were in a position to help young people grow personally and spiritually and find their place in the faith community as active Catholic Christians with a mission.

As the style of youth ministry changed, the traditional ministry to young people by the community evolved into a fourfold approach. Youth ministry was conceived not only in terms of responding *to* the unique social and developmental needs of young people but also in terms of adults' sharing a common ministry *with* young people, *by* young people (especially involving their peers), and *for* young people (adults interpreting young people's legitimate concerns and acting as advocates for them). This fourfold understanding—to, with, by, and for—changed the style and broadened the scope of youth ministry.

In 1975 and 1976, hundreds of youth leaders from across the country consulted for fifteen months and concretized the aims and philosophy of youth ministry in a document called *A Vision of Youth Ministry*. It has served to guide the church's mission to young people ever since. *A Vision of Youth Ministry* affirmed the growth that had taken place in youth ministry and challenged the whole church to renew itself.

The document clearly places youth ministry within the framework of the mission and ministry of the church. It defines youth ministry as the "response of the Christian community to the needs of young people, and the sharing of the unique gifts of youth with the larger community."[1] This reciprocal relationship helps the community to view youth ministry as part of the entire ministry of the community, not separate from it—a problem often encountered when a ministry with young people is perceived as a club or an organization set apart from the mainstream of church life. *A Vision of Youth Ministry* makes clear that an effective ministry with young people incorporates them into the life of the community, where they can share their gifts and talents with the whole community. If young people are to have positive experiences of church life, they must have opportunities to be involved in the whole life of the community. Such opportunities for this type of interaction are at the heart of youth ministry, not on the periphery. By being involved in church life with adults, young people gain a view of what it means to be an adult Catholic Christian. This is a special gift of adults to young people.

The categories of youth ministry as outlined in *A Vision of Youth Ministry* closely parallel the fundamental ministries of the church: word, worship and celebrating, creating community, and service and healing.[2] The seven categories of youth ministry describe the forms that this ministry should take. It is a common framework for a holistic ministry with young people. Briefly, the seven components of youth ministry are as follows:[3]

Word: proclaiming the Good News that leads young people to faith in Jesus (evangelization) and deepening young people's faith in Jesus and applying that faith to their everyday life (catechesis)

Worship: celebrating relationships in community and with the Lord through a variety of worship experiences, personal prayer, and spiritual development

Creating community: building relationships with young people and creating a healthy environment for growth, in which young people can experience acceptance, belonging, and participation

Guidance and healing: responding to young people's need for spiritual, moral, and personal counseling; vocational guidance; and reconciliation with self, others (peers and family), and God

Justice and service: educating young people to the demands of justice and the social problems of our world, responding to young people who suffer injustice, and motivating young people for service on behalf of others

Enablement: calling forth adults and young people to become ministers and providing them with the understanding and skills needed for effective ministry

Advocacy: working on behalf of young people, interpreting their concerns and needs, and standing up for them in the Christian, and larger, community

Youth ministry has experienced a renewal within the U.S. Catholic church. A renewed ministry with young people brings a need for new and better resources to assist leaders. Before turning to the resources found in this book, let's examine the place of creative social and learning strategies within youth ministry.

Creative Strategies for Youth Ministry

We have already seen the primacy of relationships in youth ministry. However, as relationships grow and programs are created, strategies are needed to accomplish youth ministry's tasks. The strategies in this book are aids. Their aim is to provide you with a variety of activities you can use in any number of programs. Some of these strategies are primarily suited for one or another component of youth ministry. However, most are adaptable to any number of components. All these strategies foster a particular type of learning—experiential learning. To understand its contribution to your youth ministry, let's examine experiential learning.

Experiential Learning

We have often heard it said that we learn from experience. This is true to an extent. But so much of our own life experience goes by without our ever learning from it. If young people's life experiences are to be sources of learning and growth, then young people must reflect upon and assimilate them. This often goes undone because no one takes time to help them reflect upon and learn from those experiences. In addition to life experience, there is a second source of experiential learning: structured experience. Experiences we develop that engage young people in the learning process and enable them to reflect are a rich resource for learning.

The structured experiences found in the Creative Resources series—communication games, learning strategies, simulations, projects, case studies, planning ideas, crowd-breakers, mixers, games, special events, and skits—are potential learning experiences for young people.

Creative Gaming

Creative games can serve many purposes in youth ministry. They can acquaint people with one another, build trust, encourage spontaneity, mix and blend groups, and help people release energy. At the same time, they can be fun and learning experiences. Through creative games we discover an opportunity to play *with* instead of *against* one another, thus allowing us to play as a unit and reach a common goal. This type of play lets us learn from and laugh at our mistakes, instead of hiding them away in embarrassment. Creative games enhance the growth of a group and create a feeling of accomplishment among the participants, while providing an enjoyable experience for them.

Cooperative Versus Competitive Games

For many years, competition-winning has been the name of the game in our society. All our organized sports are competitive, sometimes violently so. We encourage good sportsmanship and working together as a team, but the goal is always "Beat the other team, as badly and as hard as possible." It sometimes appears that the biggest and the best players actively compete while the meek and the mild people take their places in the stands, cheering for the physical prowess of those who are "better" than they. Competition can foster an "I am a winner" or "I am a loser" self-concept in people.

Many young people suffer from a poor self-concept. "I am too short to play basketball," "I am too heavy to run track," or "They only like me because I can make fifteen points a game" are statements we often hear from young people. "Winners" and "losers" alike may be scarred by such stereotyped images of themselves. How many adults do we know who still hold on to their childhood dream of being a pitcher in a World Series game or a quarterback in the Super Bowl? Those dreams will most likely never come true for them because they "just aren't good enough." At least that is what they believe after numerous "failures" on the field at the hands of those who are a little faster, can jump a little higher, or are more agile. Just as many adults do, many young people dream of someday "making it" and harbor an image of themselves as inadequate.

There are appropriate times and places for competitive games of basketball or volleyball, but these games may not be suitable for a break at a retreat. They may be inconsistent with the message and the values we are trying to communicate to young people.

Competitive sports can, and often do, alienate some people who might otherwise participate in group activities. Competitive games are difficult for some people and are often segregating. We see boys playing on one field and girls playing on the other. Sexism in recreation can be a divisive factor in the broad set of values we try to communicate.

For the most part, the games in this book are cooperative in character.

Principles for Cooperative Gaming

1. Games are an effective educational tool. The primary purpose of games and play is to have fun. However, we do learn during play. We learn what is and what is not acceptable behavior, for example. When young people take part in a sport, they also watch the spectators. Their observations may tell them that certain language or actions are appropriate or that others are inappropriate and may even warrant penalties. In cooperative sports, young people learn how to work as a unit, how to cooperate with one another to achieve a desired goal.

Creative sports teach us new and exciting things about ourselves and others. We learn the advantages of working together instead of trying always to win. We learn the place of healthy competition by working together. Putting competition in its proper perspective becomes an insightful experience. Cooperative games teach us skills and encourage leadership, and they enable us to grow while learning.

2. Games are an extension of the values we communicate. In cooperative gaming, we remove the element of competition and replace it with the value of working together. If caring and sharing are values we are trying to communicate to young people, then a cooperative game allows those values to be lived out even in play. There is no competing, no trying out for teams, no choosing of captains; no one is left out. No one is more important than anyone else because everyone is a vital part of the unit.

If we are trying to build community with young people but encourage competitive sports during recreation time, we contradict ourselves immediately. Cooperative games are an extension of our values: we respect each person, we work together, we have fun, and no one gets hurt.

3. Cooperative games build community and help us minister to one another. Cooperative games build a sense of community among participants. By working together and tapping one another's gifts and strengths, people discover new relationships.

Ministry happens during playtime: We encourage one another, work together, laugh, struggle, and ultimately succeed *together*. Often, the people who are ministered to during cooperative sports are those who have been left to sit in the stands before because "they weren't good enough to play." The "stars" are also ministered to because they don't feel the pressure of having to produce "points." They can play, cooperate, enjoy, be encouraged, and struggle along with the group.

4. Cooperative games encourage leadership. In cooperative play, no one is *appointed* leader because he or she is stronger, bigger, or brighter. Leadership is granted by the group, at the pace of the group, and when the need is recognized by the members. Leadership emerges by consensus, and it often develops nonverbally. Cooperative recreation encourages leadership and allows it to grow and be fostered by the group members. There is perhaps nothing more exciting to watch than the dynamics of interaction in cooperative games as young people try to conquer the obstacle at hand—and experience delight in their accomplishment. Cooperative play opens up the exciting possibilities of working as a unit, getting along, and complementing one another, as well as having fun.

5. Cooperative gaming allows the development of skills. Many people playing cooperative games have a difficult time until someone says, "I don't feel we are listening to one another. If we talk one at a time and listen, we will be able to figure this out more quickly." As the group discovers more effective means of communicating, it develops a sense of problem solving and decision-making, skills that are important to growth.

6. Cooperative games allow everyone to feel a sense of importance and accomplishment. Cooperative games allow everyone to play and work together. People are not left out because they are too short, too fat, too slow, or the "wrong" sex. Everyone is given the opportunity to feel accepted and needed instead of fearing rejection or the pressure of having to prove something to the group. *Everyone* is included in the activity. Everyone is an important part of the group and is needed by all because of the variety of experiences, personal strengths, gifts, and talents each person brings.

Guidelines for Creative Gaming

1. Always encourage and affirm the participants during games.
2. Model the Christian behavior you are expecting or hoping for from the participants.
3. Avoid games that are sexist, that is, games that assume and promote sexual stereotypes or that use sexist language.
4. Play games that challenge participants to grow, but do not choose games that frustrate the players by their difficulty.
5. Be prepared—have all equipment on hand.
6. Play only games that you personally have "field-tested."
7. Play games that help create a relaxing, comfortable atmosphere; that build community; and that avoid liable risk of bodily harm.
8. Avoid games that misuse things (such as food), waste or harm natural resources, or damage clothing, carpeting, and so on.
9. Clearly explain the object and the rules of a game before beginning (except, of course, in games that require an element of surprise).

Notes

1. United States Catholic Conference (USCC), *A Vision of Youth Ministry* (Washington, DC: USCC, Department of Education, 1976), p. 4.

2. For a contemporary description of the fundamental ministries of the church, see James Dunning, "About Ministry: Sharing Our Gifts," *PACE* 8 (1977) and *PACE* 9 (1978).

3. USCC, *A Vision of Youth Ministry*, p. 7.

PART 1

Crowd-Breakers

Introduction

The games in this part are intended primarily as initial get-acquainted activities, either for groups in which most of the people are strangers to one another or for groups where smaller groups or cliques know each other pretty well but are not comfortably acquainted with other individuals or cliques. Most of these games also have the effect of relieving nervous energy and putting young people at ease in an unfamiliar environment.

Search Me

For this crowd-breaker, give each person a sheet of paper, a pencil, and an envelope containing a small object such as a rubber band, a paper clip, a bread wrapper tie, a soda pop can tab, a nail, a piece of string, and so on. Ideally, each person should be given a different object, but duplicates are okay.

Next, explain that when you turn off the lights, each player is to place the object somewhere on himself or herself so that it is *visible* yet inconspicuous. Turn off the lights for about a minute.

When you turn on the lights, have the participants move around the room and visually search each person for his or her object. Caution them to use only their eyes for their search. Explain that when they discover an object on someone, they should write down that person's name and the object. Announce a time limit (this will depend on the number of participants, but make it challenging). The winner is the one who finds the most objects and lists each one with the right person's name.

Abbreviated Phrases

Here is a challenging quiz that can be photocopied and passed out to your group. It can be done individually or in teams—with the young people pooling their brainpower to come up with the correct answers. Each abbreviated phrase contains letters that represent words and a number that gives meaning to the phrase. (Clue: In most cases, **the number is the primary clue for figuring out the phrase.**) Set a time limit; ten minutes should be long enough.

Answers
1. 10 Years in a Decade
2. 666: The Mark of the Beast
3. 7 Wonders of the World
4. 54 Cards in a Deck with Two Jokers
5. 60 Seconds in a Minute
6. 26 Letters in the Alphabet
7. 99 Bottles of Beer on the Wall
8. 52 Weeks in a Year
9. 11 Players on a Football Team (in Canada, 12)
10. 4 Quarters in a Dollar (or 4 Queens in a Deck)
11. 3 Men in a Tub
12. 12 Apostles of Jesus
13. Rise and Fall of the 3rd Reich
14. 10 Commandments Given to Moses
15. 40 Years in the Wilderness
16. 73 Books in the Bible
17. 31 Flavors at Baskin–Robbins
18. 5 Smooth Stones in a Slingshot
19. 12 Months in a Year

Abbreviated Phrases

1. 10 Y. in a D. _____

2. 666: The M. of the B. _____

3. 7 W. of the W. _____

4. 54 C. in a D. with T. J. _____

5. 60 S. in a M. _____

6. 26 L. in the A. _____

7. 99 B. of B. on the W. _____

8. 52 W. in a Y. _____

9. 11 P. on a F. T. _____

10. 4 Q. in a D. _____

11. 3 M. in a T. _____

12. 12 A. of J. _____

13. R. and F. of the 3rd R. _____

14. 10 C. Given to M. _____

15. 40 Y. in the W. _____

16. 73 B. in the B. _____

17. 31 F. at B.–R. _____

18. 5 Smooth S. in a S. _____

19. 12 M. in a Y. _____

Bob Bob Bob

Here is a fun way to learn everyone's first name quickly. Stand in the center of the room and ask everyone to be seated in a circle or to scatter casually around the room. Move around the group randomly pointing at different people. As you point at a particular person, encourage the rest of the group to chant that person's name over and over again loudly and in rhythm, for example, "Bob! Bob! Bob! . . ."

Keep the activity going at a rapid clip. Point to everyone and keep the group chanting as loudly as possible. Encourage the group to clap in time. Point to some people more than once, point quickly back and forth between two people, and so on. It is a simple idea, but it's really wild and a great activity for learning names.

How Embarrassing!

Give everyone a sheet of paper and a pencil. Have them take a couple of minutes to write down their most embarrassing moment. Caution them to conceal their identity, to write only the truth, and to write something that they are willing to reveal to the group.

Collect the papers and read the stories to the group one at a time. After reading each one, ask the young people to guess the identity of the writer. To settle on the most likely writer, call for a show of hands. Afterward, the actual writer can reveal his or her identity. It's good for a lot of laughs, and it's an excellent way to break the ice at an informal small-group gathering.

You can substitute "my most embarrassing moment" with other ideas, like "Few people realize that I . . ." or "Ten years from now, I will be . . ."

Sum Fun

Divide the group into teams of two or more and give each team a copy of the "Sum Fun" page. Direct the team members to pool their knowledge and enter the correct number by each clue. Then have the teams add up the numbers and report their total. The team that first gets a correct total wins. Pocket calculators can be provided to make the addition a little easier, or outlawed to make it a little tougher.

Answers

1. 26	9. 90	17. 1,000
2. 7	10. 8	18. 29
3. 12	11. 4	19. 64
4. 54	12. 24	20. 40
5. 9	13. 1	21. 20,000
6. 88	14. 5 (or 9)	22. 5
7. 13	15. 57	23. 9
8. 18	16. 11 (in Canada, 12)	

Total: 21,574 (or 21,579 or 21,578 or 21,575)

Sum Fun

_____ 1. letters of the alphabet

_____ 2. wonders of the world

_____ 3. signs of the zodiac

_____ 4. cards in a deck (with the jokers)

_____ 5. planets in the solar system

_____ 6. piano keys

_____ 7. items in a baker's dozen

_____ 8. holes on an official golf course

_____ 9. degrees in a right angle

_____ 10. sides on a stop sign

_____ 11. quarts in a gallon

_____ 12. hours in a day

_____ 13. wheels on a unicycle

_____ 14. digits in a zip code

_____ 15. varieties in Heinz

_____ 16. players on a football team

_____ 17. words that a picture is worth

_____ 18. days in February in a leap year

_____ 19. squares on a checkerboard

_____ 20. days and nights of the Great Flood

_____ 21. leagues under the sea

_____ 22. days in a work week

_____ 23. digits in a social security number

_____ **Total**

Keys to the Kingdom

If you are in a big church, chances are good that somewhere in the church there is a box or a desk drawer that has dozens of old keys in it and that nobody knows which keys go with which locks. Here is a solution to that problem. Pass out the keys to your group and give the young people fifteen minutes to see how many keys they can match up with a lock in the church. Whoever matches the most keys—or any key, for that matter—can be declared the winner.

   Caution: Before doing this activity, be sure *some* of the keys actually unlock something. You may need to plant one or two. Also be sure to gather *all* the keys afterward. Security is often a problem on church premises.

Up, Up, and Away

Hang some balloons from the ceiling so that they are about seven feet off the floor. The distance can vary, depending on the height of the people in your group, but be sure the balloons are just beyond reach. Select two contestants of about the same height to compete in this event. Give them each a hat that you have rigged up with a straight pin or a thumbtack sticking out the top. Use baseball hats (or something similar) that can be adjusted to fit most heads.

   The object is to see which person can pop the most balloons by jumping up and sticking the balloons with the pin on the top of his or her hat.

Human Bingo

Here is a fun way to break the ice and learn everybody's name. Give each person a copy of the following bingo card and a pencil. Direct the players to fill in the squares with the names of people who fit the various descriptions. Each person they find must sign her or his own name in the appropriate square. The first person to complete five blocks in a row yells "Bingo."

Human Bingo

Find people who fit the descriptions found in the squares. Then have them sign their first name in the square that describes them. A person can sign your bingo sheet only once. Two winners will be declared: the first person to get five signatures in a horizontal, vertical, or diagonal line and the person who has the most signatures at the end of the time limit.

has a beauty mark	owns a dog	is wearing contact lenses	is a foreign-exchange student	owns a motorcycle
has three brothers	is going bald	has red hair	got an *A* in English	just ate at McDonald's
has blond hair at least twelve inches long	is an amateur photographer	Sign your own name.	has been to Canada	weighs less than 100 pounds
plays football	likes to jog	is wearing blue socks	drives an imported car	owns a horse
was born outside of the United States	plays guitar	played tennis over the weekend	has a cowboy hat	has a pet bird

Icebreaker

This activity takes the idea of an icebreaker literally. Have the young people sit in a circle (on the floor or around a table) with a bucket of ice cubes. Tell the group that the first person to give his or her name is to place an ice cube in the middle of the circle and that everyone else should add an ice cube as they give their name. Each cube must go on top of the previous cube. Emphasize that the object is to make the stack as high as possible.

The name sharing can be done in a variety of ways. One good way is to have each person give her or his name using an adjective beginning with the same initial as in the name (e.g., "Gallant Gary"). Then as each person gives a name in succession, he or she must repeat in order all the names previously given, without making a mistake.

Zip Zap

Zip Zap is a circle game for learning first names. The participants must know who is seated to their left and to their right. The person on their left is their "Zip." The person on their right is their "Zap." The leader stands in the center of the circle. He or she points to a person and says "Zip" and begins counting. That person must shout the name of the person to his or her left within the count of five. If the leader points to a person and says "Zap," that person must shout the name of the person to his or her right. If the person fails, he or she takes the role of leader and comes to the center of the circle, and the former leader takes the empty chair.

Shirt Sharing

This is a great group-building activity for a retreat or another occasion. It is a unique way for young people to learn some facts about one another.

You will need enough white T-shirts for everyone and a plentiful supply of felt-tip markers. Clear a work area and have the young people put sheets of paper inside the shirts to absorb the ink that soaks through. Instruct them to write or draw a variety of things on their shirt. Use these suggestions or come up with a dozen or so of your own:

1. Write your first name somewhere on the front.
2. Write your last name below the back collar.
3. Write your height in your favorite color.
4. Draw an animal that you would like to be.
5. Draw an eye the same color as yours.
6. Identify your favorite musical instrument.
7. Write your birthdate on the sleeve.
8. Draw the logo of your favorite sports team.
9. Identify your favorite food.
10. Write a Bible verse that you can quote from memory.

After the young people have finished, have them wear the shirts and direct them in a number of get-acquainted activities. For example, have them gather with others who have the same animal drawn on their shirt. Or have them take a pencil and paper and try to make a list of everyone's name and birthdate. Announce that whoever has the longest list by the end of a specified time limit is the winner. You can probably think of other games like this to play. Or the young people can just wear and enjoy the shirts.

Oddball

This hilarious crowd-breaker works best when you have an audience and a stage or a defined front area. To begin, select four or five contestants to compete in "an exciting new game." Ask them to leave the room so that they are not able to hear the rest of the group.

Place end-to-end two or three tables of uniform width. Cover them with old blankets to give the appearance of one long table. Cut a hole in one of the blankets and have a person kneel or sit between two of the tables so that his or her head sticks through the hole and above the tables. Next, place seven or eight balls of various kinds along the length of the tables. Then cover all the balls and the person's head with towels. Warn the group not to reveal to the contestants what is going on.

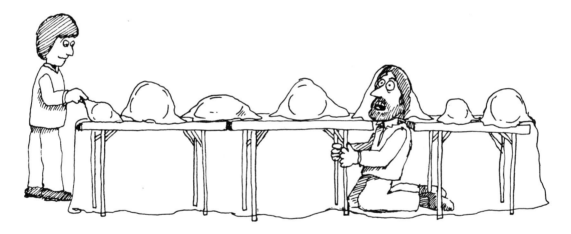

When you are ready to go, you can play the game with your contestants in a couple of ways:

1. Name That Ball: Have one contestant come into the room. Introduce him or her and encourage the crowd to cheer wildly. Explain that a number of different kinds of balls—volleyballs, footballs, soccer balls—are on the table. Tell him or her that the object of the game is for the contestant to start at one end of the table, tear off the first towel, and identify the kind of ball before proceeding to the next one. Appoint a timekeeper to clock the contestant. Announce that the winner will be the one who identifies the balls accurately in the least amount of time. Encourage the crowd to cheer on the contestant. When the contestant tears off the towel covering the head, the person between the tables should yell "Boo!" with his or her eyes bugging out. Nine out of ten contestants will jump right out of their socks. Have the contestant face the audience, because the reaction is what makes this so hilarious. Invite the next contestant in and assign a new timekeeper. Continue in this way until all the contestants have played.

2. Guess That Ball: Use the game show motif described above, but this time have the contestants *guess* what is under each towel. Tell each contestant at the start that he or she cannot touch the balls but must guess what each ball is before taking the towel off to see if the guess is correct. The contestant with the most correct guesses wins. If a correct guess is made, the crowd cheers; if wrong, they boo. It is important that the person under the towel stay perfectly still.

Time Bomb

Make a "time bomb" by placing a travel alarm clock inside a small gift-wrapped box with a removable cover. On the cover tape these instructions:

"You have just been handed a time bomb. It is set to go off. Hear it ticking. The only way you can get rid of it is to introduce yourself to a stranger in the room, tell that person where you are from, and find out the person's name and where he or she is from. Then you may hand that person this gift."

Five minutes is usually enough time for introductions before the alarm goes off, but this will vary depending on the size of the crowd. You can use more than one bomb for a large crowd. When the alarm goes off, whoever is caught with the bomb should be marked with a Band-Aid on the forehead and must be seated in the middle of the room. The victim can then reset the alarm for a shorter period of time and pass it to someone to continue the introductions. Continue this activity for about fifteen minutes.

The Why Game

On slips of paper write, "I like my church because _____." Have the group sit in a circle. Distribute one of the slips and a pencil to each person and instruct the young people to write a single phrase completing the statement.

When they have written their phrase, have them pass their slip to the person on their right. Now instruct them to write a sentence or phrase to rhyme with the sentence on the slip that has been passed to them. Then collect the slips and read them aloud.

Some of the completed rhymes will be serious, and some will be foolish, but all will be interesting.

Number Nonsense

Here are a couple "tricks" that are easy and fun to do but that will seem baffling to the people in your youth group and make you appear to be a genius. Try these sometime just for fun. It is best to memorize the procedures and carry them out as if you do this all the time.

1. Choose a number: Suggest that someone in your group (or the entire group) choose a number between 10 and 100. You must not be told this number. Use these directions to find out what the number is. (The number 44 is used as the secret number in this example.) Direct the individual or group to do the following:

- Double the secret number 88
- Add 1 89
- Multiply by 5 445
- Add 5 450
- Multiply by 10 4,500

  (tell this number aloud)

Then you subtract 100 from the result without saying anything (100 from 4,500 is 4,400). Next, strike off the last two digits (00) and announce the number (44!). Practice this a few times with your family and friends.

2. When was I born? Announce that you can guess the age and the month of birth of anybody in the group. Select a volunteer. Give her or him a pencil and a sheet of paper and the following instructions:

- Write down the number of the month you were born (August) ... 8
- Double it 16
- Add 5 21
- Multiply by 50 1050
- Add your age (16) 1066
- Subtract the number of days in a year (365) 701

You call for the result and secretly add 115, making the total 816. The first one or two digits indicate the month, and the last two indicate the age. Immediately announce August as the month of birth and 16 as the age.

Fuzzy Photos

Collect a number of 35-mm slides of recognizable objects, places, or people. Show them to your group, but begin by showing them terribly out of focus. Slowly bring each picture into focus and see who can be first to identify correctly the person, place, or thing in the slide.

The secret is in your previewing the slides, carefully choosing those that give odd effects and have misleading shapes when out of focus. Cartoons make good choices, as well as pictures from magazine ads. You will also need to practice *slowly* bringing slides into focus in a smooth motion. This activity is great fun.

The Wave

The Wave is a popular cheer at sports events in large stadiums across the country. Usually the people in one section of the stadium begin the wave by jumping up, throwing their hands up in the air, and letting out a cheer. The next section follows suit, and this continues all around the stadium in a kind of domino effect. (Trivia buffs will be interested to know that the Wave is said to have originated at the University of Washington.)

The Wave can also be done on a much smaller scale. If you have an auditorium full of people, divide the group into two sections, and try it by rows. Have the first row in each section begin by standing up and letting out a cheer. Have the second row follow, then the third, and so on, to the last row. Tell the participants that when the wave reaches the last row, they should send it in the reverse order to the front. See which side can complete the wave first.

With smaller groups, have the young people do the Wave one *person* at a time. Set it up to go down rows of chairs or around a circle. It really looks crazy when done around banquet tables.

License Plate Name Tags

Give the young people blank "license plates" (paper or cardboard in the shape of vehicular plates) and felt-tip markers. Give them time to design their own personalized license plates (like those you see on the road: KLULESS, N LUV, SWEET16, etc.). Encourage them to use creative combinations of numbers or letters. Limit the number of digits and letters that can be used on the plate to six or seven.

Allow the young people to share the significance of their plates' messages. Give prizes for the most original, most humorous, most creative, and so on. The plates can be worn as name tags for the rest of the event.

What's the Meaning?

Try these word puzzles with your group. Do them individually or in teams. The object is to decipher each word picture. Give a prize to the person or the team with the most correct answers.

Answers

1. double standard
2. tip-top shape
3. crossed eyes
4. double take
5. banana split
6. rough edge (or jagged edge)
7. several options
8. Rejoice in the Lord.
9. He spoke to them in parables.
10. Go down, Moses.
11. whosoever believes in me
12. Believe in the Lord Jesus Christ.
13. victory over sin and death
14. justification by faith
15. narrow way
16. sunny

What's the Meaning?

1 STANDARD STANDARD	2 *TOP* SHAPE	3 **✗**	4 TAKE TAKE
5 BAN ANA	6 **EDGE**	7 OPTIONS OPTIONS OPTIONS	8 LOREJOICERD
9 BULL He spoke to them BULL	10 M O S E S	11 MWHOSOEVER BELIEVESE	
12 THE LORD BELIEVE JESUS CHRIST			13 VICTORY ――――― SIN DEATH
14 JUSTIFICATION/FAITH	15 WAY	16 E	

Name Search

This game helps people who do not know one another to become familiar with the names of everyone in the group. Give each person a pencil and a word-search puzzle that has every person's name hidden among the letters. Direct the young people to circle as many group members' names as they can find (see example). Because they have to know everyone's name to complete the puzzle, they need to walk around and meet everyone.

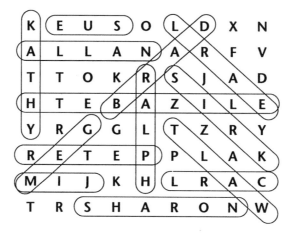

Hang It on Your Beak

With a package of plastic teaspoons and a little practice, you will break up your crowd in no time! First, practice hanging a spoon on your nose. It works if you rub the oil off your nose, breathe heavily on the inside of the spoon, and hang it on the end of your nose.

After you teach your crowd this trick, start some competition:

■ See who can hang a spoon off his or her nose the longest.
■ See who can get the spoon off the nose and into his or her mouth— using only his or her tongue.
■ See who can hang a spoon off any part of his or her face or arms.

Award comic prizes to the winners. Also bring along some spoons of varying sizes and styles and let the participants try them on for size.

Sticker Faces

This get-acquainted activity is great for large groups. Write each person's name on a pressure-sensitive sticker (round ones work best) and distribute the stickers at random. Have everyone take the label they receive and stick it somewhere on their face. Then direct each player to find his or her own name on someone else's face and stick it on his or her own shirt, blouse, or dress. Direct these two players to stay together until both have found their own name. This is a good way for the young people to see a lot of faces in a short time.

For Your Eyes Only

One of the ongoing problems with youth group meetings is how to occupy participants who show up a bit early. One solution is to hand out the following memo as the young people arrive.

For added atmosphere, seal each memo in an envelope marked "confidential" and have the theme music from a James Bond movie playing in the background.

Of course, you will need to hide the chocolate bar well enough to keep the players looking for a reasonable amount of time. For example, conceal it in a pocket of one of the leaders so that its outline is visible to the careful "detective." The lie mentioned in the memo can be anything you want. Be creative. You can adapt this idea any way you like—it works!

For Your Eyes Only

Top Secret!

Urgent!

Confidential!

Mission: The *final* and *complete* elimination of zits.

Your Task: Our government, in conjunction with other governments around the world, has declared *total war* on zits.

Our department's ongoing task in this vital effort is the total elimination of *chocolate bars* from the face of the earth!

Our intelligence has advised us that a *chocolate bar* has found its way into our church building and is hiding in open sight somewhere on the main level. We have been able to verify that it definitely is *not* in any of the offices or washrooms.

I want you, personally, to hunt down and *destroy* this fiendish *chocolate bar,* in whatever manner you deem best. You have until exactly _____ o'clock to achieve this.

Our intelligence has been able to determine that if the *chocolate bar* is not found by this deadline, it will turn itself in at the gym, to be *destroyed by me.* Therefore, regardless of results, you are to report to the gym *no later than* _____ o'clock for your next assignment.

Oh, one other thing—agent 003 was able to get some vital information to us. With his dying breath, he told us that *one* of the statements above is a lie. Unfortunately, he died before he could give us any further details.

Memorize and destroy this memo! Good luck, 007.

Oh, No!

Here is a fun mixer for your next meeting or social event. Give everyone the same number of tokens—marbles, poker chips, clothespins, or whatever. Then allow the young people to mingle and talk to one another.

Explain that whenever someone says either the word *no* or *know,* they must give one of their tokens to the person with whom they are talking. It is difficult to avoid saying those two words in normal conversation, so this game produces lots of good laughs. Give a prize to the one who collects the most tokens.

Name Tag Autographs

This is a good mixer for people who do not know one another very well. Make an eight-inch-square name tag for each person. In the middle write the person's name but leave plenty of empty space. When you are ready to begin, give each person *someone else's* name tag and have them find the person who belongs to it. After they have found that person, direct them to pin or hang the name tag on him or her. Once they have their own name tag, have the young people go around the room meeting people and having each person autograph their name tag. After ten or fifteen minutes, stop and give a prize to whomever has the most signatures.

Word Puzzles

The young people in your group will enjoy trying to solve these word puzzles. Each puzzle represents a common saying or phrase. Give a prize to the person who solves the most word puzzles within a ten-minute time limit.

Answers

1. spreading the Gospel
2. upper room
3. frankincense
4. mixed messages
5. too much of a good thing
6. not enough money to cover the check
7. stretching the truth
8. smokestack
9. three-piece suit
10. eggs over easy
11. fly in the ointment
12. sign on the dotted line
13. sideshow
14. pie in the sky
15. feeling under the weather
16. splitting the difference
17. fancy footwork
18. to be or not to be
19. bouncing baby boy
20. slanting the news
21. condensed books
22. It's a small world.
23. skinny-dipping
24. A bird in the hand equals two in the bush.
25. scrambled eggs
26. That's beside the point.
27. hanging in there
28. flat tire

Word Puzzles

1 G o s p e l	**2** **room**	**3** CENFRANKSE	**4** EMSEASSG MEGASSSE SAMEGESS GEMASSES MEASEGSS
5 a good thing a good thing a good thing a good thing a good thing a good thing a good thing a good thing a good thing a good thing a good thing a good thing a good thing	**6** **MONE✔**	**7** truth	**8** smoke smoke smoke smoke smoke smoke smoke
9 S UI T	**10** **EGGS** **EASY**	**11** OINTFLYMENT	**12** ....SIGN........
13 SHOW	**14** **SPIEKY**	**15** THE WEATHER FEELING	**16** **differ ence**
17 *FOOTWORK*	**18** BBORNOTBB	**19** baby boy	**20** **NEWS**
21 **BOOKS**	**22** WORLD	**23** D I P P I N G IN THERE	**24** HABIRDND = BUTWOSH
25 GSED	**26** T H A T 'S .	**27** IN THERE	**28** TIRE

Story-Song Skits

Remember the records we listened to as children? We played them over and over until we knew every word. Here is a way to use all those old familiar story-songs and get a good laugh with your youth group.

Divide your group into several smaller groups and give each group a cassette player and a recording of one of these children's songs. (If necessary, check the children's section in local record stores for songs. The cornier, the better!) Also, see if you can provide props.

Direct the groups to pantomime their entire song—music, speaking parts, narration, movements. Give them enough time to assemble their props and to practice. Then have the groups present the story-songs. The result is great! To ensure plenty of long-lasting laughs, videotape the performances.

Musical Showdown

This activity is great for total group involvement. Break the group into several teams and assign each team a number. Give each team a pencil and paper and several minutes to write down some songs that they all know.

When the teams are ready, shout out the number of a team and give them five seconds to start singing a song. At any point in the song, blow a whistle and shout out the number of another group. That group must start singing a different song within five seconds. To add excitement and a little confusion to the game, shout out the name of the team that is already singing, causing them to switch songs. Teams can be disqualified for these reasons:

■ singing a song that has already been sung
■ not starting a new song within five seconds
■ having less than half the group singing the song

Continue until all but one team is eliminated. Groups may add songs to their list during the showdown. To limit the song options, you might choose a particular theme, such as Christmas songs, fun songs, or hymns.

Identity

As the group enters the room, have each person fill out a name tag and drop it in a basket. After everyone has arrived, have them stand in a circle. Pass the basket around and have each person take a name tag without letting anyone else see the name. If anyone draws their own name, they should return it and draw again.

Then have everyone pin the name tag they drew on the back of the person to their left. They are to discover the name pinned to their back by asking people questions that can only be answered yes or no. For example, "Do I have red hair?" or "Am I wearing jeans?" They can ask only two questions of each person they meet.

When the players discover whose name they have, they must go to that person, place their hands on his or her shoulders, and follow that person around the room. As more people discover their partner's identity, the lines of people with hands on shoulders will lengthen until the last person finds the identity of his or her partner.

Another way to play this game is to use stickers (adhesive labels) rather than name tags. Rather than putting the names on one another's backs, they are placed on one another's *foreheads*. This makes it possible to look at the person one is speaking to.

Cross 'em Up

This game could be used as part of an evening of quizzes, for retreats, for youth meetings, or anytime you need a get-acquainted activity. Have each person write on an index card his or her name and one thing about himself or herself that not everyone knows. (You might need to do this ahead of time, perhaps at registration or an informal gathering.) Collect the cards and use the information for clues to create a crossword puzzle, with the participants' first names as the answers in the puzzle. (Many computers have a crossword puzzle program that makes this project easier.)

When it is time to play the game, hand out pencils and copies of the puzzle. Then let the young people mix freely, asking one another questions. The first one to complete the puzzle wins.

Mother Goose in the News

Below are a number of "newspaper headlines" that correspond to familiar Mother Goose rhymes. See how many of them your young people can recognize. Distribute pencils and copies of the "Mother Goose in the News" (page 34) to the group and give them about five minutes to work. Give a prize to the winner.

Answers

1. Little Polly Flinders
2. Peter, Peter, Pumpkin Eater
3. Three Blind Mice
4. Little Miss Muffet
5. Jack Sprat
6. Humpty Dumpty
7. Baa, Baa, Black Sheep
8. Sing a Song of Sixpence
9. Hark, Hark, the Dogs Do Bark
10. Tom, Tom, the Piper's Son
11. Old King Cole
12. Old Mother Hubbard
13. A Diller, a Dollar, a Ten O'Clock Scholar
14. Pease Porridge Hot
15. The Queen of Hearts
16. Rub-a-Dub-Dub
17. To Market, to Market
18. Hey, Diddle, Diddle
19. Jack and Jill (or Ding, Dong, Bell)
20. Mary, Mary, Quite Contrary
21. Jack Be Nimble
22. Georgie Porgie
23. Little Bo-peep
24. Mary Had a Little Lamb
25. Little Boy Blue
26. Pussy-cat, Pussy-cat
27. Little Jack Horner
28. A Tisket, a Tasket
29. See, Saw, Sacaradown
30. This Little Pig

Mother Goose in the News

1. Mother Disciplines Daughter Astraddle Cinders _____
2. Pumpkin Shell Solves Marital Problems _____
3. Farmer's Spouse Attacked by Rodents _____
4. Girl Terrified by Spider _____
5. Married Couple Eats Heartily _____
6. Men and Mounts Fail to Revive Crash Victim _____
7. Wool Supply Sufficient, Inquiry Reveals _____
8. Unique Pie Served Royalty _____
9. Dogs Herald Pauper's Appearance _____
10. Pig Thief Punished _____
11. Command Performance by Violinists _____
12. Poverty Strikes Home: Dog Starves _____
13. Pupil Queried About Tardiness _____
14. Appreciation of Porridge Varies _____
15. Tart Thief Repents _____
16. Scoundrels Bathe Together _____
17. Swine Sale _____
18. Animals Display Human Actions _____
19. Accident Occurs at Well _____
20. Girl Grows Garden _____
21. High Jump Skills Displayed _____
22. Amorous Advances Rejected _____
23. Lost Lambs Distressing _____
24. Lamb Incites School Riot _____
25. Bugler Sleeps on Job _____
26. Cat Tours London _____
27. Christmas Pie Reveals Character _____
28. Multicolored Hamper Appealing _____
29. Directions to London Given _____
30. Swine Tour, Eat, and Weep _____

PART 2

Mixers

Introduction

The games in this part are designed to help people become better-acquainted. They go a step beyond the initial get-acquainted, ice-breaker games that are well-known by anybody who works with young people. They can be used by youth groups whose members know—or think they know!—one another quite well. Of course, they can also be used by groups of strangers. And do not overlook this: These games can become a means of introducing young people who have been aware of one another for a long time but who have never gotten around to (or taken the risk of) deepening their relationship. This is your opportunity to be a friendship-builder. Also use these games to reshuffle old groups, comfortable cliques, or boyhood or girlhood bunches. It is all right to hang around with the old gang, but it is nice to meet new folks, too. Some of these mixers work best with large groups and others seem best for small groups. All are adaptable to your needs.

Accident Report

Give each person a pencil and paper. Ask the participants to bump shoulders with someone close when you give a signal. After they do so, direct them to file accident reports containing each other's name, address, phone number, grade, driver's license number, and so on. Give the signal six or eight times throughout the evening's activities, having the participants bump into someone new each time. This mixer is a sneaky way to compile a calling and mailing list among the participants.

Match Cards

This is a great way to help the people in a youth group get to know one another better. Give each person three three-by-five-inch cards (or slips of paper). Have everyone write something about themselves on each card. (Tell them *not* to put their name on the cards.) Suggested topics could be these:

- the most embarrassing thing that ever happened to me
- my secret ambition
- the person I admire most
- my biggest hang-up
- what I would do if I had a million dollars

Collect the cards and redistribute three to each person. Check to see that no one has their own cards. At a signal, have everyone circulate and ask questions in order to match each card with a person. Whoever correctly matches their three cards first wins. Let all the players finish; then have them share their findings with the rest of the group.

Group Up

This game is similar to both Birth-Month Bunch (page 49) and Clumps Tag (pages 51–52). Invite the entire group to mingle and move around the room. Explain that when you yell a shared characteristic, such as "first initial of first name," everyone must quickly get into groups of people who have that same characteristic. Allow a few seconds for people with the same first-name initial to gather. Then blow a whistle. The group with the most people in it is the winner.

When everyone understands the game, begin in earnest. Other possible shared characteristics are the following:

- number of people in your immediate family
- month of birth
- favorite color
- color of shirt
- age
- grade in school
- community you live in

Balloon Pop

This is not only a good mixer but also a good way to choose couples for a game that requires couples. Give each of the people in half the group a pencil, a slip of paper, and a balloon. Have these people write their name on the paper, put it inside the balloon, and blow up and tie the balloon. Direct them to put the balloons in the middle of the room. Tell the rest of the participants that at a signal they are to grab a balloon, pop it, read the name on the piece of paper inside, locate the person whose name they have, and sit down on the floor with her or him. The last couple to locate each other can be awarded a booby prize.

Confusion

This is an excellent mixer for any occasion. Give each person a pencil and the following game sheet or one that you have created. Usually this exciting and active game lasts five to ten minutes. The object is to complete each task as quickly as possible. The first person to finish the entire sheet is the winner. Expect plenty of organized confusion.

Confusion

1. Get ten different autographs (first, middle, and last names) on the back of this sheet.

2. Unlace someone's shoe, lace it again, and tie it. The person initials here: _____

3. Get a hair over six inches long from someone's head. (Let him or her remove it!) He or she initials here: _____

4. Get a girl to do a somersault. She initials here: _____

5. Have a boy do five push-ups. He initials here: _____

6. Play Ring Around the Rosy with three other people. All three initial here: _____ _____ _____

7. Do twenty-five jumping jacks and have someone count them off for you. The counter initials here: _____

8. Say the Pledge of Allegiance as loudly as you can with two other people. One of them initials here: _____

9. Leapfrog over someone wearing white shoes. He or she initials here: _____

Signatures

This mixer can be used with any age-group. It is easy and fun to play. Pick a word or a phrase associated with a holiday or the occasion of the meeting. For example, for a Christmas party, the phrase might be "Merry Christmas." Write the letters down the left-hand side of a sheet of paper and run off copies for the players.

Give each person a copy of the game and a pencil. At a signal, have the players try to find someone whose first or last name begins with one of the letters in the key word or phrase. When someone is found, they are to sign their name next to the appropriate letter. The first person to get signatures next to all the letters wins. If no winner emerges after a specified period of time, stop the game and declare the winner to be the person with the most signatures.

Name Guess

On slips of paper, write different names of famous people (one name per slip) and pin one to the back of each person. Tell the participants to try guessing who their famous person is by asking people questions that can be answered only yes or no. They may ask only one question per person. The first person to correctly guess wins. However, continue the game until everyone has guessed correctly.

People Bingo

Create People Bingo playing cards (a grid of twenty-five blank squares, five across, five down). Randomly select the names of enough people in your group to fill in each square on the card. Write the names on slips of paper and put them in a hat. Give every player a blank playing card. Give the players time to write somebody's name in each square. When everybody is ready, draw names from the hat. If a player has an announced name on her or his card, he or she is to mark an X through that name. Whoever has a horizontal, vertical, or diagonal row of X's wins.

Getting to Know You

Give everyone in the group a pencil and a copy of the following chart or one of your own devising. The object of this game is to get others to sign boxes containing descriptions that truthfully describe them. The first person to get all the boxes signed or, after a reasonable time, the one with the most boxes signed wins. A person can sign more than one box if more than one description truthfully describes him or her.

Ask the winner to read to the group the signers and the descriptions they signed. This ends the game on a funny note. To be inclusive, you might ask people who did not win to read one or two of the names of their signers and descriptions.

Getting to Know You

Find people who fit the descriptions found in the squares. Then have them sign their first name in the square or squares that describe them.

prefers Coke over Pepsi	is madly in love with someone in this room	thinks his or her sex appeal (on a scale of one to ten) is about an eight	plays guitar
has initials that spell a word	runs daily	is good-looking but not conceited	wants to be president of the United States
has seriously considered starting a house-hold recycling program	has a brother or a sister in the school choir	is not afraid of the dark	thinks going to school is time well-spent
has a pleasant-sounding voice	is wearing a hat	plans to be famous someday	has brown eyes

Permission to reproduce this page for use with your group is granted.

Seven Beans

This mixer works best with a big crowd. Give everyone seven beans. Announce a ten-minute time limit. Have the young people walk around the room asking one another questions. Explain that every time a player gets another player to answer a question with a yes or a no, he or she wins a bean from that player. Give the person with the most beans a prize.

I'd Like to Know

Do you want your group members to know one another better? Give everyone a sheet of paper and a pencil. Have them write their name at the top of the sheet. Then instruct them to write the following sentence-starter underneath their name:

■ One thing I really like about you is . . .

Then tell them to write the following phrase halfway down the sheet:

■ A question I have always wanted to ask you is . . .

Now have everyone exchange papers, notice the name at the top of the sheet they have received, and finish each of the two sentences. Have everyone exchange sheets several times so that each sheet has many affirmations and questions. When the sheets are returned to their owners, give the young people a few minutes to read what others wrote. Then have them, one at a time, read aloud and answer one question asked of them. Even if the young people know one another pretty well, there are bound to be some surprises.

Name That Person

Here is a good game that helps the young people get to know one another better. Divide the group into two even teams and appoint a spokesperson from each team. For larger groups, create four teams and have a play-off with the two winning teams and the two losing teams.

Give everyone a blank three-by-five-inch card (or piece of paper) and have them write down five little-known facts about themselves and sign their name. For example:

1. I have a pet snake.
2. My middle name is Hortense.
3. I was born in Mexico City.
4. I hate pizza.
5. The carpet in my bedroom is green.

Collect all the cards, keeping each team's stack separate. Explain that the object is to "name that person" using as few clues as possible. Begin by opening the bidding between the teams: "We can name that person in five clues!" "We can name that person in four clues!" and so on.

Let the team that wins the bidding guess first. Draw the top card from the other team's stack and read aloud as many clues as the team bid on. Announce a five-second time limit, beginning after you read aloud the clues. The team members can huddle to come up with an answer. The more interaction among them, the better. If the team fails to guess the person or if they do not respond in five seconds, the point or points go to the other team.

The scoring goes like this:

■ five points for one clue
■ four points for two clues
■ three points for three clues

- two points for four clues
- one point for five clues

To avoid the teams' guessing the person by the process of elimination, return to the card piles those cards the teams have failed to guess. If the cards are drawn again, read a clue or clues that have not been read yet. Proceed until every card has been used at least once. Total up the points and announce the winner. Award gag prizes if you wish. After the game has ended, you can read the rest of the clues that are on the cards (clues that have not been read yet), and if the original guess was wrong, you can let the whole group try to guess again—just for fun.

Match Up

Here is a fun game that really gets people talking with one another. On index cards, type or write the statements below in the following way: Put each statement, except the word or words in italics, on the left-hand portion of an index card. Put the words in italics on the right-hand portion of the index card. Make sure that as you type or write, you use a larger part of card for the longer phrase. Then cut the index card in two (see illustration).

Here is a list of statements (you may want or need to add phrases of your own):

- I always eat bacon with *eggs.*
- Tarzan lived in the jungle with his wife *Jane.*
- We could save on gasoline with fewer *jack-rabbit starts.*
- Banjo players never die; they just lose their *pluck.*
- What good is a peanut butter sandwich without *peanut butter?*
- People in glass houses shouldn't throw *stones.*

Randomly hand out the portions of the index cards. Instruct the players to find the match to their card by doing the following:

- introducing themselves to someone
- holding their card next to the other person's card
- reading aloud the resulting sentence

Some combinations can be very funny. If two people think they have a match, they must have a leader check it. If they have a correct match, tell them to sit down and watch.

A variation is to give everyone a large and a small portion of cards that do not match and make them find a match for *each* portion.

Let's Get Acquainted

Make copies of this list of twenty directions and give one copy to each person in the group. The first person to find and write in the names of the people who fit the descriptions wins. You may want to devise a list that betters fits your own group. Be creative.

Let's Get Acquainted

1. Find someone who uses Listerine. _____

2. Find someone who has three bathrooms in his or her house. _____

3. Find someone who has gotten more than two traffic tickets. _____

4. Find someone who has red hair. _____

5. Find someone who gets yelled at for spending too much time watching television. _____

6. Find someone who has been inside the cockpit of an airplane. _____

7. Find someone who plays piano. _____

8. Find someone who likes to eat frog legs. _____

9. Find someone who has been to Hawaii. _____

10. Find someone who uses your brand of toothpaste. _____

11. Find someone who has used an outhouse. _____

12. Find a boy with a ring. _____

13. Find a girl who has gone waterskiing and got up the first time. _____

14. Find someone who knows what *charisma* means. _____

15. Find someone who is on a diet. _____

16. Find someone who uses a Remington shaver. _____

17. Find someone who has a movie ticket stub. _____

18. Find someone who has his or her own private phone at home. _____

19. Find someone who doesn't know your last name. _____

20. Find someone who has an unusual-sounding last name. _____

Oddballs

This mixer can be adapted for use with almost any size group. Make copies of the following list or a list of your own devising. Before the game begins, have ten boys and ten girls prepare themselves to fit the descriptions on the list and caution them to keep their descriptions secret until the game begins. To begin the game, give each person a pencil and a list of the descriptions. The first person to find and write in the names of the people who fit the descriptions wins (the twenty "oddballs" are eligible to play and win too).

Oddballs

Girls, you must find the boy who . . .

1. has a red comb in his back pocket _____

2. has a rubber band around his sock _____

3. has his wristwatch on upside down _____

4. has his shoes on the wrong feet _____

5. has a thumbtack on the heel of his right shoe _____

6. has a bobby pin in his hair _____

7. has a Band-Aid on his neck _____

8. has his shoe laced from the top down _____

9. has on only one sock _____

10. has his belt on inside out _____

Boys, you must find the girl who . . .

1. has on one earring _____

2. has a rubber band around her wrist _____

3. has on mismatched earrings _____

4. has a brown shoelace in a white shoe _____

5. has lipstick on her ear _____

6. has a paper clip on her collar _____

7. has nail polish on one fingernail _____

8. has a ruler in her pocket _____

9. is chewing bubble gum _____

10. has on one nylon stocking _____

Whopper

Use this game with groups whose members know one another fairly well. Give everyone a piece of paper and a pencil. Direct them to write four things about themselves—three must be true, and one must be a *whopper* that is disguised to sound true. (Make the true statements little-known facts so that the whopper sounds true by comparison.)

As each person reads his or her list to the group, the rest should try to guess which statement is the whopper. (Do not let the reader reveal the whopper until everyone has guessed.) Keep score this way: Whoever guesses correctly gets a point. The person whose list is being read gets a point for each incorrect guess.

As a variation, have the players create three whoppers and one true statement. Have the rest guess which statement is true.

Coin Bingo

Have the young people bring a dollar's worth of change and play this version of bingo. Give each person a game sheet (page 45). Then have the group mingle and find people who have the coins described on the sheet or who can answer the questions or perform the task correctly. Tell them to ask the people who supply the help to initial their respective squares. The first person with five initialed squares and correct answers in a row (vertically, horizontally, or diagonally) wins.

The game can also be played individually by allowing players to use only the coins in their possession to fill in the spaces. Adapt the rules to make the game harder or easier, according to your situation.

Positive People Bingo

Try this version of bingo at your next social or party. It works especially well for people who are familiar with one another and whose members could use some affirmation. Give each person a pencil and a copy of the bingo sheet (page 46).

Coin Bingo

Find people who have the coins described on this sheet or who can answer the questions or perform the task. Have them initial the appropriate square.

a nickel minted between 1980 and 1985	a game token	a penny made before 1950	What does *e pluribus unum* mean?	a half-dollar
exactly thirty-seven cents in change	a dime minted between 1985 and 1990	a quarter with a small *d* on it	What is the name of the building on the penny?	four quarters
a quarter that is more than twenty-five years old	Whose picture is on the quarter?	a foreign coin	a nickel minted between 1951 and 1955	a 1989 penny
seventeen pennies	five dimes	Which president is on the dime?	exactly sixty-three cents in change	a penny, a nickel, a dime, and a quarter
six coins of the same denomination	a silver dollar	no quarters	a 1976 quarter	Flip heads three times in a row.

Positive People Bingo

Find people who fit the descriptions found in the squares. Then have them sign their first name in the square that describes them. A person can sign your bingo sheet only once. Two winners will be declared: the first person to get five signatures in a horizontal, vertical, or diagonal line and the person who has the most signatures at the end of the time limit.

is a good friend	has a good sense of humor	has helped me before	has a nice smile	has leadership qualities
is a sweet person	has good ideas	is easy to talk to	is a fun person	is understanding
is an encourager	cares about others	is someone I would like to get to know better	is talented	is friendly
is a strong Christian	is loving	has a gentle spirit	seems happy with self	is patient
is kind	is a good person	is kind of crazy in a good way	is creative	makes me feel good about myself

Permission to reproduce this page for use with your group is granted.

PART 3

Games

Introduction

This part, the largest in the book, provides a wide array of games for all seasons and all places under the sun—and for all places under the roof, too, for that matter.

To help you find your way, the games fall under four separate headings:

- Indoor Games for Large Groups
- Indoor Games for Small Groups
- Outdoor Games for Large Groups
- Outdoor Games for Small Groups

These categories are not airtight. For example, if you have an open-gym night in January for a group of twenty young people, you will naturally want to begin looking under the heading "Indoor Games for Small Groups," but don't stop there. Use your imagination and ingenuity and check out the games under the other headings. The games described in this part are quite adaptable.

Take a minute now to review the section "Creative Gaming," in the introduction to this book. This is just to remind yourself of a few ground rules and procedures. Happy gaming!

Indoor Games for Large Groups

The games in this section are best played indoors with groups of thirty or more. Since most of them require quite a bit of space, play them in a gymnasium or a large recreation room.

Many of these games are easily played outdoors and can also be played with smaller groups.

Balloon Basketball

Divide the group into two teams of equal size. Arrange rows of chairs so that in each row the opposing team members face one another.

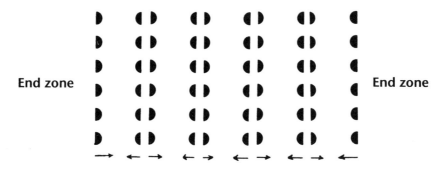

Have the players be seated in their team's chairs. Toss a balloon into the center of the players. They must remain seated as they use their hands to bat the balloon to the end zone that they are facing. When the balloon drops into an end zone, the team facing that end zone wins two points. If the balloon goes out-of-bounds (i.e., anyplace out of the players' reach), throw it back into the center.

Play can continue to twenty points or may end after fifteen minutes.

Balloon Stomp

Have the players use string to tie a balloon around one of their ankles, leaving about ten inches between the ankle and the balloon. Tell the players to try to stomp and pop everyone else's balloon while keeping theirs from being popped. The last person with an inflated balloon is the winner.

Math Scramble

Divide your group into teams. Have each person wear a piece of paper with a number on it. Each team should be given an identical set of numbers, and the numbers should begin with zero. Send the teams to separate parts of the room and stand equidistant from each team. Tell them that you will shout a math problem, such as "2 times 8 minus 4 divided by 3," and each team must send the person wearing the correct answer (in this case, the person wearing the number 4) to you. Point out that no talking is allowed—the people with the correct answer must simply get up and run. The first person to get to you wins one hundred points for their team. The first team to reach one thousand points (or whatever) wins.

Birth-Month Bunch

Give each person a list like the one below or simply make copies of this list. Instruct the players to look at the action described for the month of their birthday. Tell them that when the lights are turned out, they are to immediately carry out the behavior that corresponds to the month of their birth. Explain that as soon as they find a person doing the same thing, they are to lock arms and look for others who share their birth month until all the birthday bunches are complete.

Birthday Actions

January—Shout "Happy New Year!"

February—Say "Be My Valentine."

March—Blow like wind.

April—Hop like the Easter Bunny.

May—Say "Mother, may I?"

June—Say "Will you marry me?"

July—Make fireworks sounds.

August—Sing "Take me out to the ball game."

September—Fall down repeatedly.

October—Shout "Boo!"

November—Say "Gobble-gobble."

December—Say "Ho Ho Ho, Merrrry Christmas!"

Line Pull

Divide the group into two equal teams. Have the teams stand facing each other on either side of a line drawn on the floor. The object of the game is for each team to pull the other team's members across the line into its territory. Alert team members that they may not move farther than two feet behind the line and that they may not step over the line. If they do, they must join the opposing team. At the end of an announced time period, the team with the largest number of players wins.

Blind Sardines

This noncompetitive game is good with large groups. Appoint one person to be the sardine. The sardine may or may not wear a blindfold (your choice). All the other players must wear blindfolds. Explain the game:

- The objective is to come into contact with the sardine.
- When one player touches or bumps into another, he or she grabs the other player and asks, "Are you the sardine?" The sardine must answer "yes" if asked.
- Once a person finds the sardine, she or he becomes a sardine and must hang onto the other sardine for the remainder of the game.
- Eventually more and more players bump into the sardines (who must identify themselves as such) and add themselves to create a sardine chain. The game is over when everyone has become part of the sardine chain.

Four-Team Dodgeball

For this fast-moving game, divide the group into four teams of equal size. If you have a basketball court marked on the floor, use this as the playing area; otherwise, mark off your own boundaries. Divide the floor into quadrants:

Assign each team to one of the four areas and caution them not to leave their assigned area during the game. Use a volleyball, a beach ball, or a kick ball (a basketball is too hard). The rules are basically the same as those for dodgeball, with these exceptions:

- Players may throw the ball at anyone in any of the other three quadrants.
- If a player is hit below the belt with the ball, she or he is out of the game.
- If the ball goes out-of-bounds, the referee tosses the ball to the team in whose quadrant the ball went out-of-bounds.
- If a player catches the ball before it hits the floor, the player who threw it is out.

The winning team is the one with the most players left at the end of a specified time limit.

Broom Soccer

Arrange chairs in an oval, with an opening at both ends. Divide the group into two teams of equal size. Assign each team one of the two open ends of the oval as its goal. Have the teams sit on opposite sides of the oval and tell each team to count off separately.

To begin, have the 1s come to the center and give each a broom. Toss a rubber or plastic ball into the middle of the oval. The two players are to use their broom to try to knock the ball through the opponent's goal. As referee, you can shout a new number anytime. At this point, the two players in the center must drop the brooms, and the two new players are to grab the brooms and continue. Play continues as long as the ball is in the oval. If it is knocked out-of-bounds, return it into play. Make sure the players in the chairs understand that they cannot interfere with the ball with their hands, but they may kick it if it is hit at their feet.

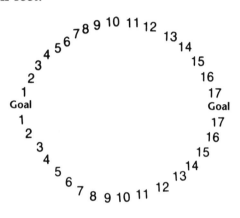

Chain Tag

This fast-moving game can be played indoors or outdoors. One person is designated as "It," and her or his job is to tag people. When she or he tags someone, the two of them join hands and continue tagging people as a unit. Once eight people are in the group, they must break apart and become two groups of four. As the game continues, several groups of four end up chasing the free single players. The game is played until everyone is caught. Running in groups is a lot of fun, and the effect is something like crack-the-whip.

Clumps Tag

This great game combines tag with Anatomy Clumps (see page 77). It should be played in a space that has boundaries, like a large room or a basketball court. One person is "It." The leader should have a referee's whistle.

The game begins with everyone milling around, including the person who is It. As soon as the referee gives the whistle two or more short blows, It begins to tag people. (If a PA system is available or if the referee can shout loud enough, the referee can simply shout the appropriate number rather than use a whistle.) The players avoid being tagged by getting into clumps of people equal in size to the number of blows on the whistle. For example, if the referee blows the whistle three times, people try to get into a group of three and lock arms. Anyone who is in a group of three cannot be tagged. The person who is It has approximately thirty seconds to tag as many people as possible. At the sound of one long whistle, everyone starts milling around again, safe for the moment. The referee then blows the whistle again a certain number of times, and again everyone trys to get into a group of the appropriate size and lock arms. The game continues in this manner. Extra people are almost always running around madly without a group and its safety. Those people who are tagged leave the game, and the winner or winners are those people left when time is up.

For larger groups, you might want to have more than one It. A good idea is for It to have a crazy hat, shirt, or something else that will help everyone identify her or him.

Birthday Races

Divide the group into teams of equal size. On the signal "go," have each team line up according to their date of birth, with the youngest person on one end of the line and the oldest on the other. The team that rearranges itself most quickly wins. For round two, have them line up by birthday (regardless of age), with those whose birthday is closest to 1 January at the head of the line.

Toe Fencing

Set this game to music; it will look like a new kind of weird dance. Have all the players pair off, hold hands, and try to tap the top of one of their partner's feet with one of their own feet. Because players are also trying to avoid having their feet stepped on, they will all hop around the floor in a frantic dance.

Tell the players that when a partner has had her or his foot tapped three times, she or he is out of the game, and the winning partner must pair up with and challenge another winner. The game continues until only one person is left or until the music runs out.

Garbage-Bag Ball

For this game, take a large, plastic garbage bag, fill it with inflated balloons, and tie it. You now have a garbage-bag ball. Ask the players to take off their shoes. Have all but ten of your group form a large circle and kneel. Have the remaining ten players form a pinwheel formation in the center of the circle, lying on their back with their head toward the center.

The object is for the players who are on their back to kick or hit the ball out of the circle, over the heads of the players in the outer circle. The outer circle will try to keep it inside the circle. If the ball is kicked or hit over the head of a player in the outer circle, that defender must take the kicker's place in the inner circle.

Toss the garbage-bag ball into the circle. Play for as long as you wish.

Another game you can play with a garbage-bag ball is Garbage-Bag Volleyball, using regular volleyball rules.

Speller

Give everyone a large letter of the alphabet to wear. If you prefer, mark a letter on each person's forehead using a washable marker. Avoid the use of little-used letters like *Q*, *X*, and *Z*.

After you have given the players time to mingle, blow a whistle and shout a number. The players must find other people with whom to form a word from the same number of letters as the number called. For example, if you call "Three," a person with the letter *A* might join with a *T* and a *C* to spell *cat*. (Keep the numbers small enough so that words can be formed.) Any players who are unable to become part of a word within a reasonable amount of time are out of the game.

Pull Up

For this game, everyone is seated in a circle, on chairs or on the floor, except for five girls and five boys who are in the middle. This number may vary depending on the total size of the group.

Each of the ten players in the middle run to someone of the other sex who is seated in the circle, grab her or his hand, pull the player up, and take her or his place in the circle. A person who is pulled up runs to the other side of the circle, pulls up someone of the other sex, and takes her or his place in the circle.

The game continues until the leader blows a whistle; then everyone who is up freezes instantly. The leader counts the number of boys and the number of girls who are up. If more boys than girls are up, the girls get a point. If more girls than boys are up, the boys get a point. In other words, the team with the fewest people standing wins points.

Crazy Basketball

Divide your group into two teams (they do *not* have to be equal in size). Play the game on a regular basketball court but without regular basketball rules. In this game, anything goes. The object is to score the most baskets in any way possible. Players can run, pass, dribble, or throw the basketball with no restrictions. For example, players can ride piggyback for height. This game plays best with fifty to one hundred participants.

Indoor Scavenger Hunt

Divide the group into teams. Stand in the middle of the room and have each team get into a separate area of the room. Give each team a minute to appoint a runner. Tell the teams that you will name various items that might be in the group, and each team is to locate that item and give it to the runner, who will run it to you. Announce that the first team to produce an item wins one hundred points, and after twenty or so items, the team with the most points wins. Make sure that all the runners are running approximately the same distance. Here are some sample items you can call for:

a white comb	a stick of gum
a red sock	a theater ticket
a 1979 penny	a picture of your mother
a student ID card	a hat
an eyelash curler	fingernail clippers
a white T-shirt	a store receipt
a shoestring (without the shoe)	a cowboy boot
four belts tied together	exactly forty-six cents
dark glasses	a handkerchief
a picture of a rock star	a Timex watch
a twenty-dollar bill	a book with no pictures
some beef jerky	a turquoise ring or bracelet

Shuffle the Deck

Here is a simple, lively game to break a large group into smaller ones or to play just for fun. Distribute one playing card to each person in the group. Call out different combinations, like these:

■ Get in a group that adds up to fifty-eight (an ace equals 1; a jack, 11; a queen, 12; and a king, 13).
■ Find three other people who have your suit.
■ Get in a group of five cards in a row, of any suit.

- Find your whole suit.
- Find three other people with your number.

For larger groups, use multiple decks of cards; for smaller groups, eliminate cards.

Sing-song Sorting

Do the following ahead of time:
- Decide how many teams you want to play with (they should be equal in size, but it is not essential to the game).
- Choose a different but well-known song for each team.
- For each team member, prepare a slip of paper with the team's song title on it. For example, if you have one hundred participants and you want four teams, prepare twenty-five slips for each of four different songs.

As each person enters the room, give him or her (at random) one of these song titles. Explain that at a signal, the lights will be turned out, and the players should start singing their song as loudly as possible. No other sounds are permitted. Each person must try to locate others singing the same song. The first team to get together is the winner.

Weather Balloon Volleyball

Two teams of any number can play this funny volleyball game that uses a giant weather balloon for a ball. Giant weather balloons are available from army surplus stores and other specialty shops. Other types of giant balloons can also be used. It is best to play this game indoors because a light wind can carry your balloon a long way. The balloon (which inflates to six to eight feet in diameter) can be inflated with an air pump. An entire team will have to get under the ball to push it over the net.

Stack 'em Up

Prepare a list of qualifying characteristics such as these:
- If you had eggs for breakfast . . .
- If you got a traffic ticket this year . . .
- If you have striped socks on . . .
- If you are not afraid of the dark . . .

Have everyone sit in chairs in a circle. Read a characteristic and a command. If the characteristic applies to any players, they are to follow the command. For example, if you say, "If you had eggs for breakfast, *move three chairs to the right and sit down,*" all those who qualify must move as instructed, regardless of whether that chair is occupied by one or more persons. As the game progresses, players will begin stacking up on some chairs. Vary each command by changing the direction and the number of chairs.

Squirrel

For this game, everyone except two players gets into a group of four. Three of the four group members join hands and become a hollow tree. The fourth group member is a squirrel who is inside the hollow tree.

The two extra players are a squirrel and a hound. When the game begins, the hound chases the extra squirrel among the trees. For safety, the squirrel may crawl into any tree, but the squirrel already in that tree must leave and flee from the hound. If the hound tags the free squirrel, the squirrel becomes the hound, the hound becomes the squirrel, and the game continues.

Light Wars

Although young people are continually being warned not to run in the halls, give your group the run of the building just once. Play Capture-the-Flag (pages 82–83) *inside,* marking out each team's territory.

Instead of tagging the enemy to make captures, players catch an enemy player in the beam of a flashlight and call out his or her name. The "beamed" player must sit out for five minutes. Equip each player with a standard flashlight. Ban spotlights, fluorescent lights, and lights with five-volt batteries.

If the group plays several rounds of Light Wars during the evening, you might want to show one of the *Star Wars* videos at the same time for the enjoyment of players who may want to sit out a game or two.

Card Squads

Here is another variation of Capture-the-Flag (pages 82–83). You will need the standard Capture-the-Flag equipment—two flags and a big area with plenty of hiding places—as well as two decks of playing cards.

After two teams are formed and have hidden their flags, distribute to each player a playing card—a heart or a diamond to "Red" team members and a spade or a club to "Black" team members. The cards determine a player's rank—a king is higher than a queen; a queen is higher than a jack; and so on, down to the two. An ace can beat a king but loses to any other cards.

Once play begins, both teams try to capture the opposing team's flag, according to the rules for Capture-the-Flag. When a tag occurs, both players reveal their card. The player with the highest-ranking card wins and continues playing, but the losing player goes to Central Exchange—a designated central place—in order to exchange his or her card for another (of his or her team's color). Only then can he or she rejoin the game. If the players in a tag have identical rank, both must go to Central Exchange. The winner is the first team to capture the other team's flag and return it to home territory.

For variety, you can make all the ten-cards "bombs" that can "blow up" all other cards. If a card is blown up, its holder is out of the game. All the five-cards can form a "bomb squad," which are the only cards able to defeat the ten-cards.

Pass Out

This game is sure to frustrate players—that is, until they get the knack of it.

Divide the group into teams of eight to sixteen players and line them up relay style. Give everyone a toothpick to hold in their teeth. At one end of each line, have ready a Lifesaver and a Kleenex; at the other end, a seedless grape and a piece of string. Direct the team members to pass all four items from one end of their line to the other without using their hands. Explain that if they possess more than one item at a time, they must pass them in this order: Lifesaver, grape, Kleenex, string.

As the relay heats up, players in the middle will get stymied trying to figure out how, with a grape bayoneted on the end of their toothpick, they can pass a Lifesaver—or how to pass the piece of string if a Kleenex is draped over their toothpick.

Here is the secret: In a worst-case scenario, all four things pile up on a single person in the middle of the line, who has to pass them all to their correct directions. First he or she takes the Lifesaver (sliding it far back on the toothpick), then impales the grape, then grabs the Kleenex with the corner of his or her mouth, and then hangs the string on top of everything.

To unload it all, he or she passes the Kleenex one way, turns and lets another have the string, passes the grape off in the direction of its destination, and ditto for the Lifesaver. Voilà!

Basket Dodgeball

For this game you need a gym or a full basketball court, two hoops, four basketballs, and a kick ball.

The group is divided into four equal-size teams. Each team lines up in a corner of the court (see diagram) in tallest-to-shortest order. A basketball is placed by each team. Each player on the team is assigned a number—1 for the tallest, 2 for the next tallest, and so on. (To accommodate uneven teams, some players may get two numbers.) A kick ball is placed at center court.

Now to play. When all the players are sitting, the leader yells out a number, for example, "Three!" The four 3s leap up, grab their basketball, and dribble it to the basket at the opposite end of the gym. When a player makes a basket, he or she carries the ball back to his or her team and sets it down. And here is where dodgeball enters. The *first* to replace his or her basketball runs to center court, picks up the dodgeball, and begins a dodgeball game with the other 3s. Whoever he or she hits is out. (The ball must hit the person without first bouncing.) If the intended victim catches the ball, the thrower is out. (Woe to the player who is still struggling with making a basket when the other three start dodgeball!) If the dodgeball thrower is eliminated, a 3 who has made a basket and returned the basketball may be the thrower.

When three 3s are eliminated from the dodgeball part of the game, the surviving 3's team earns one point. Then balls and players return to their starting positions, and another number is called. Play continues until a team reaches a predetermined score or until time has expired.

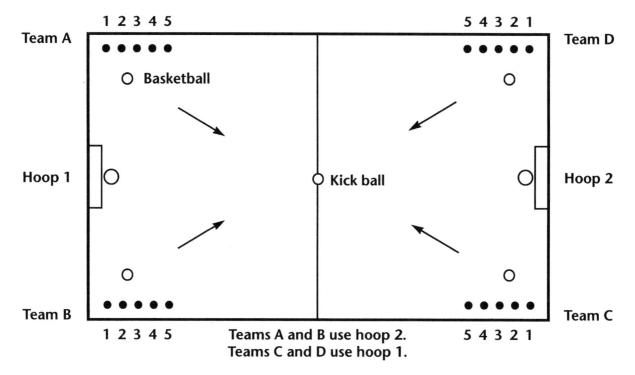

Volley Slam

This game is like baseball, but it is played on a volleyball court in a gymnasium. Form two teams of any number of players. Home plate is in the middle of the backcourt (or if your volleyball court is situated on a basketball court, under one of the baskets), and six bases are placed in the court's corners and by the net's poles (see diagram). The defensive team scatters itself throughout the gym. The batter stands at home plate and bats the volleyball with a normal underhand or overhand volleyball serve toward the far end of the court.

- Outs are made only by hitting runners with the ball when they are between bases or when a batted ball hits the net. Outs are *not* made by catching flies.
- A base may hold any number of runners, and runners may pass one another.
- If you are playing under basketball backboards, a home run is scored if a batted ball hits the backboard, rim, or net at the opposite end of

the court. Awards may be given if the ball goes *into* the basket—for that is certainly a feat!

- Because no catcher is used, a thrown ball that crosses the home-base line is out of play, so runners must remain at the bases closest to them.
- The area beyond the sidelines *and* beyond the net is still inbounds.
- The length of an inning is determined by the number of members on a team. All team members bat once and only once in each inning.

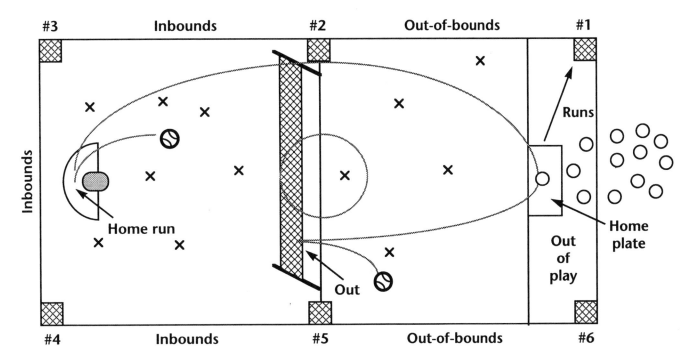

Pop Fly! Ground Ball!

The object of this indoor game for thirty or so players is to be the first of four teams to successfully throw or roll a colored Nerf ball among all its members and then back to the captain.

First, arrange chairs in a square, divide the group into four equal teams, and instruct the members of each team to sit opposite their teammates—like this:

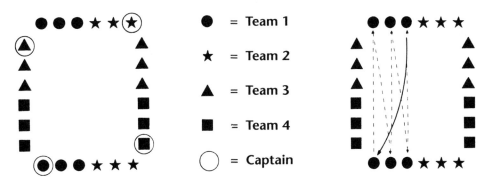

Next, give each team a different-colored Nerf ball. Ask one person on each team to act as captain. The captains must sit at the end of their team's line, and they must all sit at the same position relative to their team.

Here is how the game is played: Each captain tosses the team's Nerf ball *across* the square to a teammate opposite her or him. That player then tosses the ball back across the square to the player seated next to the captain—and so on.

At any time, the leader can yell "Ground ball!" and all teams must immediately begin *rolling* their ball across the floor instead of throwing it. When they hear "Pop fly!" they return to tossing the ball. It is permissible for the leader to yell the same signal several times in succession—just to keep the players guessing!

The last person on the team to receive the ball tosses it back to the captain, after which everyone on that team stands up and yells—thus letting everyone else know they have finished and won.

Indoor Challenge Ball

For this game you need a gym or a similar room that is nearly indestructible and that has running room. Have two teams of equal size line up on opposite sides, about three feet from the wall. Then have the team members number off.

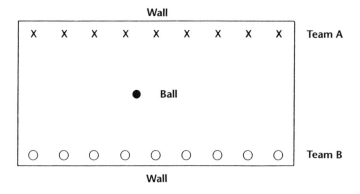

Place a ball in the middle of the room. (Any large kick ball, beach ball, or Nerf ball will do.) Tell the players that when you call a number, the two players with that number (one from each team) must run to the middle and try to hit the opposing team's wall with the ball. The team standing in front of the wall is to try to stop the ball.

Tell the players that they are permitted to get the ball to its goal any way they can—by carrying, throwing, kicking, rolling, whatever. Anything is legal. When everyone is ready, call out a number. After a few minutes, call another number, and so on.

Indoor Games for Small Groups

All the games in this section are great for playing indoors with groups of thirty or less. The games are not limited to thirty, but they are best played with small numbers. Some require a large indoor space, like a gymnasium, while others can be played in a much smaller space. Many of the games throughout this book can be easily adapted for use with small groups in an indoor setting.

Goofy Golf

Set up a miniature golf course all over your playing area. If you are using a church building, make your course travel down hallways, in and out of rooms, down staircases, and the like. Either use golf balls, balloons with a marble inside (they take unusual rolls), Ping-Pong balls, or whiffle golf balls. For clubs, use golf clubs, broom handles, rolled-up newspapers, and so on.

Put a flag by each hole and mark each tee. Set par for each hole, print up some scorecards, and let the Goofy Golf tournament begin.

Pass It On

The entire group forms a circle. Everyone is given an object of any shape or size—a bowling ball, a trash can, a shoe, and so on. At a signal, everyone passes her or his object to the person on her or his right, keeping the objects moving at all times. When a person drops any object, she or he is out, but the object remains in. As the game progresses, more people leave the game, making it harder and harder to avoid dropping an object. The winner is the last person left in the game.

Balancing Broncos

This game moves quickly and is challenging. It calls for two teams. On each team, have the girls pair off with the boys and let each pair determine who will be the horse and who will be the rider. If the number of girls to boys is uneven, have some of the girls or some of the boys play twice. The object of the game is for the horses to run a course with a rider balancing cross-legged on their back. The riders must try to balance without using their hands to hang on. It is easier if they face backward. The horses must go around an obstacle and back without their rider falling off. If the rider falls off, they must go back and start again at either the beginning or the halfway point (whichever is closest). The game is over when one team has sent all its horses and riders around the obstacle.

Balloon Blower Basketball

For this game, you will need a basketball court, two basketballs, and two large uninflated balloons. Have one team line up behind the free throw line at one end of the basketball court and the other team at the other end. Ask each team to designate a balloon blower.

At a signal, the first person in line shoots a basketball from the free throw line or dribbles as close as she or he wants and shoots. After shooting, the player throws the ball to the second person and gets back in line. The second person in line must stay behind the free throw line until the ball is thrown back by the person who just shot. Each time someone makes a basket, the balloon blower makes one giant blow into the balloon. The team that pops its balloon first wins. If you want the game to go longer, you can give each team two or three balloons.

Basketball Squat

The group is divided into teams of about six to ten people. The teams choose captains and line up in a straight line facing them. Each team is about five to ten feet away from its captain. The captain throws the ball to the first person in the line. That person returns the throw and squats down. Next the captain throws the ball to the second person, and so on. When the last person in line squats, the captain throws the ball back to that person. He or she throws to the captain and stands up, and so on, down the line. Play continues until everyone has received a second pass, thus working back to the first person in line. Any time the ball is dropped, the team must start over. The first team to get everybody standing up again is the winner.

Musical Squirt Gun

This exciting game can be played indoors or outdoors with a group ranging from six to thirty people. Have the group sit in a circle either on chairs or on the floor. Direct the group to pass a loaded squirt gun around the circle until the music stops (or until you say "stop"). The person holding the squirt gun at that time may squirt the person on his or her left or right once or twice. Then he or she must leave the game. After his or her chair is removed and the circle is made smaller, the game can continue. The last person who has not been squirted is declared the winner.

Ask the players to pass and receive the gun with two hands, otherwise it will be frequently dropped and will break. (Have a second loaded squirt gun on hand for use when the first gun is empty. You might want to have an assistant refill the original gun while the second one is being used.)

Blackout

This twist to musical chairs is a real riot. First arrange the chairs in a circle facing outward. Have the players form a circle around the chairs. Explain that the players must keep their hands behind their back. When the music starts, the boys walk around the chairs clockwise, while the girls move counterclockwise. When the music stops, participants must sit down on the closest empty chair. There is one catch—the game is played in the dark.

When the music starts, turn the lights out. When the music stops, turn the lights on. Be prepared for a lot of scrambling and running for chairs. The person left standing is out. Be sure to take one chair out after each round and move the remaining chairs closer together as the group gets smaller.

Blindman Bacon

This game requires two teams of equal size positioned in one large circle. The members of each team stand next to one another. Each team numbers off. When a number is called, the corresponding player from each team puts on a blindfold. After hearing the whistle, both players go to the middle of the circle and, with the guidance of screams from teammates, try to locate a squirt gun lying in the middle of the circle. The player who finds the squirt gun tries to squirt the other player before that opponent escapes the circle, behind her or his teammates. If the player with the squirt gun successfully shoots the other player, a point is awarded to the shooter's team. If the other player escapes, her or his team is awarded a point.

The game is made more exciting if, after the blindfolds go on, the leader moves the squirt gun, making it more difficult to locate.

Bottle Ball

This game can also be played outdoors. The ideal number of players for this game is five for each side, but it can be adapted for more. Mark on the floor distinguishable boundaries of approximately sixty feet by thirty feet. The three end players must guard two bottles each (see diagram). The bottles (large plastic soda pop bottles work ideally) in each pair should be placed about eighteen inches apart. The throwers try to shoot a medium-size Nerf ball (or another type of soft ball) through the opposite side, their opponents blocking the ball as best as they can. Players foul when they step beyond the midway line.

The scoring goes like this:

■ five points for each bottle knocked down
■ ten points for each shot that goes between the bottles
■ one point for each shot rolling over the back boundary line

The teams can be created by dividing the group into four, six, or eight different teams for a tournament.

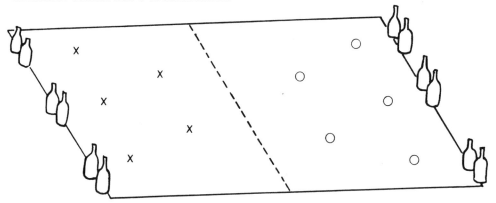

Contest of the Winds

On the floor, draw a large square divided into quadrants. Designate the quadrants North, East, South, and West. Divide the group into four teams and assign each a direction. Scatter dried leaves evenly in each quarter of the square. At a given signal, direct the "winds to blow." Each team must try to *blow* (no hands allowed) the leaves out of their square into another. Set a time limit. The team with the least leaves in their square wins.

Feetball

This active indoor game requires teamwork. Divide the group into two teams and seat them in two lines of chairs, facing one another. Place the facing chairs just far enough apart so that the opposing team members' feet barely touch when the members of both teams extend their legs. Tell the teams that the object is to move the volleyball (or a similar ball) to the goal at the end of the line by using feet only. Designate which end is the goal for which team. Have the players keep their arms behind their chair to keep from touching the ball. Have the players remove their shoes. To begin the game, drop the ball in the middle of the line between the two teams and stand back!

Dunce Bombers

Divide the group into two teams and ask them to be seated on opposite sides of the room. Ask for a volunteer from each team to be a dunce. The dunce sits near the back of his or her team with a paper cup balanced on his or her head. The players must stay seated where they are throughout the game. The object of the game is to knock the cup off the head of the other team's dunce, using wadded newspaper. The game usually takes a stack of newspaper about four feet high. Disperse the paper so players can reach it. The dunce cannot use his or her hands in any way, but his or her teammates can bat down flying paper bombs. A point is scored each time a team knocks off the other team's dunce cap.

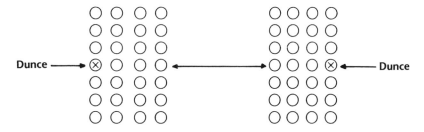

Ping-Pong Baseball

You can play an exciting game of baseball indoors using Ping-Pong balls and Ping-Pong paddles. This fast-moving game requires a large room. If the ball hits the ceiling on the fly, it is playable, but the walls are foul territory. All other baseball rules apply.

Ping-Pong Polo

For this exciting indoor game, have team members make their own polo sticks out of rolled-up newspaper and masking tape. Have them roll up several sheets of paper lengthwise and then tape the sheets along the edges. Play requires one Ping-Pong ball, but have extras on hand.

Explain that the object of the game is to knock the Ping-Pong ball into the other team's goal. (To make goal areas, at each end of the playing area, lay a table on its side with the top facing into the play-ing area. When the ball hits the table, it will make a popping noise, indicating that a goal is scored.) Have each team select a goalie. The goalie can use any part of her or his body to protect the table.

Ping-Pong Table Baseball

This indoor game works well for small groups. To set it up, you will need a card table, a Ping-Pong ball, and some masking tape. On the card table, use the masking tape to mark off the playing lines (see diagram). You need foul lines and lines that indicate first, second, and third base.

Place the Ping-Pong ball on home plate. Each member "at bat" attempts to blow the ball across the bases for a home run. The team "in the field" places three players on their knees on the opposite side of the table, and those players attempt to blow the ball off the table before a base hit is scored.

- Each batter may blow only once.
- The fielders may not touch the table.
- If the ball crosses one of the foul lines, the player at bat is allowed another blow, even if the fielding team blew the ball back across the foul line.

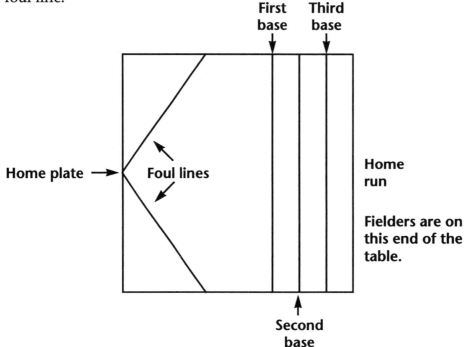

- A score is calculated at the point where the ball makes its farthest forward progress before being blown off the table by the fielders. For example, if the batter blows the ball, and it reaches the third-base tape before being blown off the table, the batter is credited with a triple. The next batter may get a double, putting two people on base—one on second and the previous batter on third. The next batter may hit a home run, which would score three runs. Runs may only be forced in.
- Outs are made by blowing the ball off the table before it reaches the first-base line and in such a way that it does not go back across the foul line.
- Home runs are made by blowing the ball off the table on the opposite end from home plate.
- Caution fielders to be careful about where they are blowing the ball; they can unintentionally score for the opposing team.

Scoop

Have the group sit in a circle. You will need a round cookie tin lid or some other circular object that can be spun on the floor. Have everyone in the circle number off and then pick one person to be "It." Explain how the game works: The person who is It spins the lid on its edge in the middle of the circle and calls a number. The lid must keep spinning long enough for It to take a seat in the circle. The person whose number is called tries to pick up the lid with one hand before it falls over. If she or he is successful, the original It comes back to the center and spins the object again. If not, the person whose number was called remains in the center as the new It.

Ha Ha Ha Game

This crazy game is good for a lot of laughs—literally. One person lies down on the floor (on his or her back); the next person lies down with his or her head on the first person's stomach. The next person lies down with his or her head on the second person's stomach, and so on.

After everyone is on the floor, the first person says "Ha," the second says "Ha ha," and the third says "Ha ha ha," and so on. This game is to be played *seriously,* and if anyone laughs out of turn, the group must start over.

Sock Ball

This version of baseball is ideal for an indoor setting. Everything used in the game is made out of socks. Stuff a long tube sock full of socks to make a bat and stuff a smaller sock to make a ball. Everyone must play in their stocking feet. On a freshly waxed gym floor, this game is a riot.

Trust Tag

In this unusual variation of tag, the players play in pairs, and one wears a blindfold. The seeing player guides the blindfolded player from behind by keeping his or her hands on the partner's waist and shouting directions. Tell the players that the object is for the blindfolded player to tag another blindfolded player. To make this game even more difficult, have the seeing teammate give his or her blindfolded partner directions *only* by pushing or pulling.

Balloon Bomb

Remember the leftover party balloon that you bounced around in the air when you were a child? That rainy day entertainment still works with youth groups today.

Formalize the game a bit. Form two teams and tell them to try to hit the balloon away from the opposition so the balloon will hit the ground before the opposition can hit it. Allow only one hit per team (i.e., no consecutive hits by members of the same team are allowed) and forbid intentional grounding—all hits must loft the balloon. Set up this scoring system:

- Intentional grounding and consecutive hits by members of the same team score a point for the opposition.
- If the balloon touches the ground, the point goes to the team that hit it last.

Try this variation: Instead of having the two teams intermingle in the playing area, put them on opposite sides of a six-foot-wide "dead zone." Permit two hits per team (by different players) before volleying the balloon across the dead zone. For more than two hits per team or more than one hit per person, score a point for the opposition. If the balloon lands in the dead zone, score a point against the team that hit it last. A team can serve until it loses a point.

Double Shuffle Toss

Arrange chairs in a circle so that everyone has a chair. Then add two extra chairs to the circle. Have everyone sit in a chair except for the player who is "It." Put her or him in the middle of the circle. Have the sitters keep moving around from chair to chair to prevent It from sitting down. As everyone shuffles from chair to chair, they pass or throw a rolled towel to anyone in the circle. If It intercepts the towel, she or he trades places with the player who threw it. The player who is It can also trade places by tagging the one holding the towel. Also if It manages to sit down in a chair, the person on her or his right becomes It, and the game continues.

For a large group, add more people in the middle, more towels, and more empty chairs.

Obstacle Ball

When a sudden rain shower threatens to dampen your recreational spirit, retreat indoors to a large room or even a smaller space for this variation on baseball. Use a foam bat and ball (available in most discount variety stores) and divide into two teams.

Now for the wrinkle. Leave a clear running lane between home plate and first base, but litter the "field" liberally with folding chairs. This prevents a hit ball from traveling very far. When the shower passes, you can move the game outside.

Bump Relay

Teams of about five to ten people are seated in chairs that are lined up relay fashion. At a signal, the first player in line leaves his or her seat and rushes along the right side to the back of the line and, with some adept hip action, "bumps" the teammate off his or her chair to the right (see diagram). The one who is bumped moves forward a chair and bumps that teammate off to the left—and so on, to the front person, who runs around to the rear of the line and starts the process over again. The first team to return all its members to their original chair wins.

Personality Pursuit

Have two hundred to three hundred small strips of paper on hand for this game. When the group arrives, have them write on each strip a person's name—others in the group, celebrities, people dead or alive, comic strip characters, and so on, as long as the name is relatively well-known. Do not worry if a name is written more than once; it makes the game more fun. Then put all these strips in a pail.

Now divide the group into two teams and explain the game: A player from team *A* draws a name from the pail. He or she has thirty seconds to give clues to his or her teammates, who must try to guess the name. Any spoken clue is permissible, and pointing is allowed. If the team guesses the name within thirty seconds, that strip is pocketed by the team for tallying later. If the team fails to guess the name, the strip goes back into the pail. After team *A* has had its chance, team *B* follows suit. Each team member should have a chance to draw a slip. At a designated time, the teams tally up the names they have guessed. The team with the most correct guesses wins.

Fuzzy Ball

This takeoff on baseball is perfect for indoors and for groups of ten to fifty. You will need a "fuzzy ball"—one of those softball-sized nursery toys with a rubber center and a fabric (usually yarn) covering—and a plastic whiffle ball bat. (In a pinch you can use a Nerf ball and a broom.) Lay out home plate and three bases (see diagram) and divide players into two teams. Fuzzy Ball rules differ slightly from baseball rules:

■ With a hit, players run to what is normally third base, then to what is normally first base, then to what is normally second base, and then home.

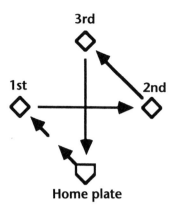

- Runners are put out only by a tag or by being hit below the shoulders by a thrown ball. Catching fly balls and tagging bases are *not* ways to get a batter out.
- Everyone on a team gets to bat once, and only once, each inning, regardless of how many outs. (Outs retire runners from base running; they do not determine the length of the inning.)
- The team at bat supplies its own pitcher; a maximum of three pitches are allowed to each batter; two strikes constitute an out.

Power Pong

First, clear the room of all breakable objects. Set up a Ping-Pong table and put out at least four paddles. Divide your group into teams. As few as two and as many as six players can be on a team. Two teams can play at a time. Serving and scoring will follow standard Ping-Pong rules. Neither players nor their paddles can cross the plane of the net.

Here are the procedural rules:
- Each side is permitted as many as three hits before returning the ball across the net. A player cannot hit the ball twice consecutively.
- Walls, ceilings, and bodies are all in play.
- If the ball touches the floor, it is dead, and the point goes to the opposition.

Teamwork makes for accurate sets and smashing returns. You better have a few extra balls for this one.

Balloon Pong

Get some balloons and play this slow-motion version of Ping-Pong. Line up the players, one team on each end of a Ping-Pong table. Play according to regular Ping-Pong rules—except use one paddle. So after a player hits the balloon, she or he must slide the paddle across the table and under the net to the player opposite her or him. When a player makes her or his shot and slides the paddle to the opposing player, she or he needs to scoot out of the way as quickly as possible and move to the end of the line.

The players may keep the balloon aloft with their breath if they need time to snatch the paddle.

Ring Net Ball

This basketball-type game is great for gym night. As in baseball, the defense scatters itself around the gym. From the sideline at midcourt, an offensive "batter" throws a basketball into the "field." He or she then runs out to the circle at midcourt—the "base"—and runs around it as many times as possible before the defense gets the ball and sinks a basket. Score one point for each completed circle around the base. Everyone on the team gets to be the batter before the inning switches.

Spin the Compliment

This game requires a soda pop bottle and a circle of players willing to affirm one another. The spinner lays a compliment or word of encouragement on whomever the bottle points to at the end of its spin.

Strobe Ball

Try playing the old, familiar games four-square or volleyball in a room lit only by a strobe light (available at electronics shops). It is surprising how difficult it becomes to keep a semblance of coordination. The young people will be swinging at balls and usually missing.

Ping-Pong Blow

Players in this game spread themselves evenly around a large bedsheet, take an edge, pull the sheet taut, keep it level, and attempt to blow a Ping-Pong ball off it. The players between whom the ball drops off the sheet are out, and the circle of players is gradually reduced.

Instead of a Ping-Pong ball, a balloon with a marble inside rolls around the sheet less predictably and makes a challenging variation.

The ParenTeen Game

This game initiates communication—both between the parents and their teenagers and among the group members themselves. It's like the old TV show the "Newlywed Game." Send the parents out of the room. Then ask the teenagers a series of questions about their parents (adapt or use the sample questions on p. 72). The young people should write their answers in large letters on a sheet of paper. Let the audience read them, but remember to hide them from the parents' view until they have responded, too. Invite the parents back in, ask them the same questions, and award points to each parent-teen team whose answers match.

Then switch—send the young people out, ask their parents a series of questions about their children, bring the young people back in, and ask them the same questions. Compare answers and again award points to each parent-teen team whose answers match. Be sensitive to single-parent homes—adjust the wording of some questions if you need to. Give credit for partially correct responses.

The ParenTeen Game: Sample Questions

Questions for Teenagers

1. Does your father prefer coffee (*a*) before a meal, (*b*) with a meal, (*c*) after a meal, (*d*) not at all. (5 points)
2. What will your parents say it costs to run the (primary) family car each month? You must come within ten dollars of your parents' answer. (5 points)
3. What will your mom say it costs to feed your family for one month? You must come within twenty dollars of your parents' answer. (5 points)
4. Where did your parents meet? (10 points)
5. Name one of your mother's good friends and one of your father's good friends. (10 points)
6. When your parents have a free hour, what does your mom like to do with it, and what does you dad like to do with it? (10 points)
7. What do you think your parents will say are the two biggest problems they face as parents of a teenager? (20 points)

Questions for Parents

1. What part of the chicken does your son or daughter like the most? (*a*) the breast (*b*) the drumstick (*c*) the wing (*d*) none of it (5 points)
2. If your daughter or son could have voted in the last presidential election, who would he or she have voted for? (5 points)
3. What is the first name of your son or daughter's best friend? (5 points)
4. Name four subjects (be specific) that your daughter or son is taking in school this term. (8 points)
5. What will your child say is her or his hardest subject? Easiest subject? (10 points)
6. What will your child say he or she plans to do after high school? (*a*) go to college (*b*) get a full-time job (*c*) get technical or vocational training (*d*) enlist in the armed forces (*e*) figure out what he or she wants to do (10 points)
7. What do you think your son or daughter will say are the two biggest problems he or she faces as a teenager? (20 points)

Up Jenkins

This game of concealment and feint is best played by small groups, even as small as six to twelve players. Get a long table, chairs for all players, and a quarter. Divide the players into two teams and have them sit on opposite sides of the table. Ask each team to elect a captain.

The game progresses this way: One team secretly passes the quarter back and forth among its members underneath the table. When the captain of the opposing team says "Up Jenkins!" all the players on the quarter-passing team close their fists, lift their arms, and place their elbows on the table. Then the opposing captain says "Down Jenkins!" and all the players simultaneously slam their hands down on the table. If this is done well, the other team won't hear the quarter hit the table.

The object is for the guessing team to eliminate all the hands that do *not* have the quarter, leaving for last the one hand with the quarter under it. So the opposing captain chooses people to lift their hand one at a time. The team with the quarter can respond to the captain only. Lifting a hand in response to anyone else on the opposing team means forfeiture of the quarter. One of the goals of the opposing team, therefore, is to trick people into lifting their hand in response to someone other than the captain.

If the opposing team's captain successfully lifts all the hands except the one covering the quarter, his or her team wins and takes possession of the quarter. If, however, the captain uncovers the quarter *before* the last hand, the quarter-passing team retains possession and a new round begins.

Once the young people get the hang of it, they will develop all sorts of strategies to make their hand look like it does not have the quarter.

Volley Feetball

This volleyball variation will keep your group light-footed. Play it according to the traditional volleyball rules, except for one big difference—lower the net to within a foot or two of the floor, and tell the players they can use only their feet to kick the ball *under* the net. Here are the rules:

- The players on both teams stand aside in order to let the serve reach the opposite team's back row by traveling *under* the net. After a back-row player has kicked it, players on both teams may move back into position and resume regular play.
- If a player in the front row of the serving team touches a served ball before it goes under the net, it is side-out—that team loses its chance to serve. If a player in the front line of the receiving team touches the ball before it reaches the back row, the serving team scores a point.
- If the back row of the receiving team lets a served ball go out-of-bounds untouched, the serving team scores a point.
- When a player kicks the ball *over* the net, of course, a point goes to the opposing team, or the ball goes to the other side.
- Games are played to seven, fifteen, or twenty-one points.

The young people may find the game a little tricky at first. They will need to kick soccer style. This game can be adapted for play in a smaller room using a Nerf ball and masking-tape boundaries.

A-maze-ing Grace

Form a labyrinth with masking tape (see diagram A). Divide your group into teams of four. The rules are simple:

- Each team of four must stand with their backs to one another, lock arms, and form a square (see diagram B). Each team member must face a different wall and remain facing that direction throughout the game regardless of the turns and the corners the team makes as it proceeds through the maze. At any given time, one player will be walking forward, another backward, one shuffling to the right, and another to the left. The quad-squad must move as a unit.
- Teams are disqualified if they rotate from their original position or disconnect arms.
- Teams are timed; the fastest team wins.
- Teams get penalty seconds if they cross the maze lines.

To avoid collisions, start the next team when the previous one has left the maze.

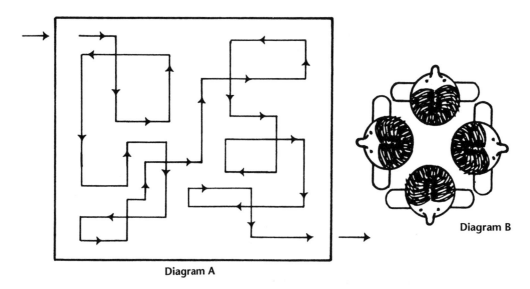

Diagram A

Diagram B

Biblical Character Stumper

Do your young people need to brush up on their knowledge of biblical characters? If so, divide your students into about four groups and designate one of them the panel. Circulate among the remaining groups, whispering to them the name of a single biblical character. Give these groups a few minutes to list factual yet obscure clues about that character. Permit them to use Bibles if they want. When everyone is ready, have the groups take turns giving the panel one clue about the character. Give the panel a few moments to consider clues before they guess.

The group with the fewest points wins the game. So whichever group gives the last clue before the panel correctly guesses is penalized and receives a point. If the panel guesses correctly following the first clue, it receives one point. If the panel takes two turns, it earns two points, and so on. The same clue can only be guessed at once. Have the groups take turns at being the panel and at giving clues about a biblical character.

WRDS

The imagination, vocabulary, and teamwork of your youth group will get a workout with this game. Give each team a list with several letter combinations on it—PMR, CRY, and SPR, for example. Challenge each team to make words that keep the letters in order. From PMR a team might make *ProMpteR;* from CRY, *unCleaRlY.* The team with the longest word wins that round—*unCleaRlY,* for example, beats *CRYing.* The winner of the most rounds wins the game.

Variation: Require that words be proper nouns, foreign words, biblical words, and so on.

Arena Nerfketball

If you have a large room at your disposal and can mount Nerf ball baskets and backboards at either end (or mount them on simple, portable frames), you can generate all the enthusiasm of a tournament play-off. Divide your group into two teams and give them time to devise team names and cheers. Have groups of five rotate in and out every few minutes so that everyone has a chance to play. Use referees to maintain order and keep the game moving. Since the baskets may be fragile, tape off the area four feet out from each basket and declare it out-of-bounds.

These rules keep the game active:
■ Players must pass after taking three steps.
■ No touching opponents.
■ No roughness.
■ Play stops at a referee's whistle, and the ball goes to him or her. Violation of this rule results in a penalty.
■ All penalties result in a free throw for the other team.
■ Free throw shooters must rotate.
■ Referees' decisions are final.

For a fitting and frenetic finale, invite *everyone* onto the floor for the game's last minute!

Double Vision Volleyball

This volleyball game is played with two balls. On the referee's command, both teams serve simultaneously. Each ball is played until a point is scored. Either team can score with either ball. A team can score *two* points from the simultaneous serve.

If necessary, to compensate for the power plays of stronger players, use plastic children's balls instead of standard volleyballs.

Movie Madness

Distribute one three-by-five-inch card to each participant and instruct him or her to write down the name of a movie, a TV program, or a commercial. Players should not see what the others have written. Collect the cards.

Divide the group into teams of four or five people and have each team draw one card from the pile. Instruct the teams to take three to five minutes to quickly plan a scene from the movie, the TV program, or the commercial that they chose. After gathering the groups together again, let the teams act out their scenes one at a time. When the performing team is finished, have the other teams guess what movie, program, or commercial was portrayed.

For extra fun, record the evening on video, edit it, and play it at your next movie night.

Two-on-Two Basketball

Here is a twist to the standard two-on-two game; it is especially adaptable to tournament play. Each two-person team designates one of its members as the stationary shooter. That person must remain at one end of the free throw line; he or she cannot move his or her feet and can only shoot for his or her team. The remaining person on each team is the moving player, who gets rebounds, blocks shots, intercepts passes, that is, does everything *but* shoot.

The variations are endless. In coed games, designate the girls as shooters, the guys as moving players. Or place your shooters anywhere on the court in order to vary the difficulty of the shots. Or add players and designate more shooters or more moving players.

Volloony Ball

This indoor volleyball game uses a balloon wrapped with three lengths of masking tape to make it heavier, faster, and more erratic (see diagram). For a net, line up chairs or run a taut string between two chairs. Have everyone get on their knees to play. Keeping score is optional; the players will have a great time just making desperate saves and keeping the ball in the air. Have a few extra balloons on hand; fingernails and spiking tend to pop them.

The Rule Game

Players sit in circles of three to six people. The only rule is that players take turns devising rules that must be followed for the duration of the game. For example, a player might say on his or her turn, "If you use a word that begins with *T*, you must stand up and take a bow." Or "If you touch your hand to your face, you must run around your chair three times." Or "Every time you break a rule, everyone must point at you and cough." And the game cannot end without (can you guess?) someone's making it a rule. This game can be adapted for long bus trips.

Anatomy Clumps

Players begin by milling around the room as the leader stands in the middle. After a few seconds, the leader blows a whistle and yells out two things: a part of the body and a number ("Elbow! Three!"). All players then rush to get into groups of whatever number was called and connect with one another at the body part that was called. After the call "Elbow! Three!" for example, players form groups of three and touch elbows with one another. The last group to do this correctly is eliminated.

Other examples of possible calls:

knee, four
nose, three
ankle, six
back, two
rear, five
neck, two
shoulder, six
head, four

Mystery Dotter

In this indoor game, a "detective" must reveal the identity of the mysterious dotter who is placing self-adhevsive dot labels on other members of the group. A dotter is selected secretly and is given enough dot labels to stick onto everyone in the room. The detective tries to do three things:
- let people know, if they are not aware of it, that they have been dotted
- keep a record of all who have been dotted (in case dot labels drop off in the course of the evening)
- identify the dotter

This kind of game can continue behind the scenes while other games are being played. If the dotter is identified, a new dotter and a new detective can be chosen, and the game can continue. The object is for the dotter to dot as many people as possible before the detective discovers her or his identity.

Letter Search

Do you want to impress on your group a key word or a short phrase for an upcoming study or lesson? Write the word, letter by letter, on one-inch paper squares. Tape these squares in obscure places in the building, for example, under the fire extinguisher, on the doorknob to the pastor's office, and so on.

When the meeting begins, give each person a pencil and a three-by-five-inch card. Tell them that they are looking for a word or a phrase, the letters of which are scattered throughout the building. Also tell the players the number of letters they are looking for. Explain that when they find a letter they should copy it onto their card, leaving the letter in place so that other players can find it, too. Tell them that after they have found all or some of the letters, they must try to unscramble them and guess the word or the phrase. Warn them to be subtle as they are hunting so they do not give away the location of letters they have already found.

Award two prizes: one for the player who finds the most letters and one for the player who first figures out the word or the phrase.

Puzzle Wrap

Here is a successful way to introduce a discussion. Ahead of time, roll out six feet or so of cling wrap on an uncarpeted floor. On the wrap, write out a biblical verse using a colored permanent marker. Cut apart the verse in jigsaw fashion. Wad up each piece into a tight ball. Repeat the process using a different color of permanent marker and a new verse. You will need one jigsaw biblical verse for each team. Mix up all the wads and put them in a sack.

At game time, dump the wads into a pile on the floor. Assign each team a color, and let them begin finding the wads and assembling their verse. The first team that completes its puzzle and reads its verse wins.

Ping-Pong Home-Run Derby

You can play this all-or-nothing version of baseball with just a handful of players, a fair-size room, a Ping-Pong ball, and a paddle (the "bat"). Set four or five folding tables on their sides as a playing-field fence (see diagram). Use masking tape to form a home plate and two foul lines.

Now for the rules:
- All players must play on their knees.
- There are no strikes, no balls, no base hits—just home runs or outs. The batting team tries to hit home runs.
- A Ping-Pong ball that clears the fence without touching the floor or the ceiling counts as a home run. If a hit ball touches the floor or the ceiling or is caught or swatted down by a fielder, the batter is out.

- Foul balls are played over.
- The fielding team, which plays along the inside of the fence, tries to swat the Ping-Pong ball down before it flies over the fence.
- Each team gets three outs.
- The number of innings to be played can be decided by the teams.
- Umpires and scorekeepers may be chosen or not.

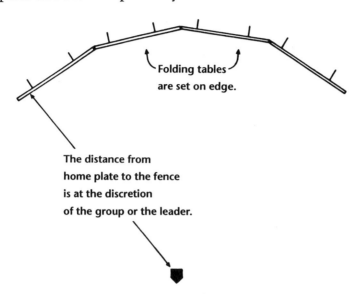

Folding tables
are set on edge.

The distance from
home plate to the fence
is at the discretion
of the group or the leader.

Ping Pool

For a full hour of fun, try this hybrid of Ping-Pong and pool. First, set up a six-foot-long folding table. Attach six paper cups along the edge of the table—one at each corner and one in the middle of each of the long sides—like the pockets of a pool table. Cut out the bottom of each cup and tape on a small plastic bag. Make a final check to see that the cups fit snugly to the table. If they do not, cut and shape them to get a tight fit.

Choose two teams of six players each and position them at random along the edge of the table on their knees with their arms folded on the table and their chin resting on their folded arms. Place on the table twelve Ping-Pong balls—six white ones for one team, six red ones for the other. (Either buy red balls or color white ones with a marker. If you do this, use a permanent marker so the color won't wear off during the game.) Announce that only two balls—of any combination—are permitted in any pocket. Act as referee to make sure this rule is followed during play. At the whistle, direct each team to blow its balls into the table's pockets. The players' arms will keep the balls on the table. Be on hand to put out-of-bound balls back into play. The team that sinks its balls first wins.

Here are some variations:

Tag-Team Ping Pool: Have only one member from each team play at a time. Ask the other team members to wait their turn in an area away from the table. When a person has successfully pocketed one ball, she or he can tag a team member, who will then represent the team at the table. The game is over when a team has pocketed all six of its balls.

Bumper Ping Pool: Scatter about ten unopened, ice-cold cans of soda pop on the playing table. Have the players blow balls around the cans of pop to sink their balls in the pockets. The winning team gets first choice of the soda!

Challenge Ping Pool: This is the same as regular Ping Pool, except that only one ball of each color may roll into each cup.

Score Ball

This variation of baseball is a great equalizer of talent—nonathletic players do as well as athletes. Mark an indoor or outdoor playing area into zones as per the diagram below. Get a bat and three Nerf balls of different colors.

Divide your group into two teams. Have the fielding team spread out in the field. Score Ball is played this way:

- A batter gets only three pitches. Three strikes put him or her out, as does a fly ball that a fielder catches.
- The three colored balls are pitched in the same sequence for each batter. The first pitch (e.g., the red ball) is worth one point if it is hit; the second (yellow), two points; the third (blue), three points. Using colored balls makes it easy to keep track of the points. A batter may choose either to hit any ball or to wait for the second or third pitch. The batter may score only once each turn at bat.
- The point value of a hit ball is multiplied by the point value of the zone it lands in (see diagram). For example, if a player hits the second pitch (two points) into the middle zone (five points), she or he earns ten points for her or his team. A hit, therefore, can earn from one to thirty points. Play as many innings as you like.

X = Defensive players

Outdoor Games for Large Groups

This section contains a variety of outdoor games for groups of thirty or more people. Some can be played with an almost unlimited number of people, but these are best played on a large, open field.

Keep in mind that this book contains many other games that can also be played outdoors with large groups, including some of those found in the indoor sections. So do not limit yourself to this section if you are looking for just the right game for your next outdoor activity.

Twin Softball

This is a good game for a group that is too large to play a regular softball game. Evenly divide the group into two teams. Have team members pair off and hook arms with their partner. At no time while playing are they allowed to unhook their arms or to use their hooked arms. They may however, use their free arms and hands. Use a rubber ball or a volleyball instead of a softball because it can be caught with the pair's free arms and hands.

When at bat, pairs are to grasp the bat with their free hands. After the ball is hit, the pair must run the bases with arms hooked together. Other than these exceptions, regular softball rules apply.

The Blob

Boundaries are clearly marked off and spotters are put on the corners. During the course of the game, players who step outside the boundaries become part of the blob.

One person begins as the blob. The blob tries to tag another player. If a player is tagged or is chased out-of-bounds, he or she becomes part of the blob. These two join hands and go after a third person, who, when tagged, joins hands and helps tag a fourth person. The game continues until everyone is part of the blob. The blob members must hold hands. Thus, only players on the ends can make legal tags.

For the blob to be most effective, it must work as a unit. One person should act as the "blob brain" and control the blob. No tags count if the blob becomes separated, so the blob must go after one person at a time. Once the blob becomes large enough, it can stretch across the playing field and catch everyone by forcing them out-of-bounds.

Bedlam

This game requires four teams of equal size. Each team takes one corner of the room or the playing field. The play area can be either square or rectangular. At a signal, each team attempts to move diagonally to the opposite corner, performing an announced activity as it goes. The first team to get all its members into its new corner wins that round.

In the first round, teams can be directed to simply run to the opposite corner, but after that use more-challenging activities, such as walking backward, wheelbarrow racing, racing piggyback, rolling somersaults, hopping on one foot, skipping, or crab walking. There will be mass bedlam in the center as all four teams crisscross.

Bedlam Elimination

This game is a variation of Bedlam. Team members gather in the four corners of the playing field, as in Bedlam, but this time each person gets a flag (like those used in flag football) that they must wear in their back pocket or in the waistband of their pants. A safe area is designated and marked off for each team. The game begins with everyone standing behind that line.

On "go," everyone races diagonally across the field to the opposite corner. On the way, the players try to grab the flags out of opposing team members' pants. A team gets a point for each captured flag, and a team member who loses his or her flag is eliminated from the game. Play continues until only members of one team are left.

Capture-the-Flag

Young people still like to play this old game. The playing field needs to resemble this diagram:

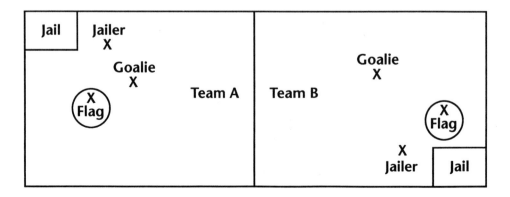

Team *A* is on one side of the field, and team *B* is on the other side. The idea of the game is to capture the flag that is located in the other team's territory, without getting tagged. Once a player crosses over the line in the middle of the field, he or she can be tagged and sent to the opposing team's jail. A player can free a jailed teammate by getting to the jail without being tagged and tagging the prisoner. Both get a free walk back to safety. Each team has one goalie, who watches the flag from a distance of about ten feet, and a jailer, who guards the jail.

Capture-the-Football

This is an exciting variation of Capture-the-Flag (see previous activity). Footballs replace flags. A team wins by passing or punting the opposing team's football over the line that separates the team's territories. If players are tagged, they must remain prisoners until teammates tag them and set them free. If the football is passed over the line and the pass is incomplete, the passer and the intended receiver both must go to jail. If the pass is complete, the team wins. Other Capture-the-Flag rules can be adapted as needed.

Power Baseball

This variation of softball allows nonathletic people and athletes to play competitively. It is especially successful with fifteen or more people on a side. To avoid the possibility of easy outs, use a tennis ball and a tennis racket. Anyone can hit a good shot, and it is almost impossible to strike out. (If you think some people will hit the ball too far, have them use a racquetball racket.)

Fat Bat

This version of softball can be played out-of-doors in any kind of weather, and anybody can play. It does not require much skill.

Purchase a fat bat and a fat ball from a toy store or a department store. These items are relatively easy to find and are quite inexpensive. Regular softball rules apply, but there are no foul balls. Every hit is fair. The ball is so light that a good wind will carry it anywhere. So the nastier the weather, the better.

Human Football

This wild game can be played on any rectangular playing field, outdoors or indoors. A football field works fine. Divide your group into two teams. When a team is on offense, it begins at its twenty-yard line. The offense gets four downs to move the ball down the field and to score a touchdown. (There are no additional first downs.) A player hikes a football to the quarterback, who is then picked up and carried by the rest of the team down the field. All of the team members must be in touch with one another as the ball is advanced, either by carrying the quarterback or by holding on to team members who are carrying him or her.

The defensive team begins each play lined up on the goal line they are defending. As soon as the offensive team hikes the ball, the defensive team locks arms and walks (no running allowed) down the field toward the offensive team, which, in turn, is moving toward the defensive team. When the defensive team reaches the offensive team, the two end members of the defense try to dislodge one of the offensive players from the rest of the team. As soon as this is accomplished, the down is over. The ball is put into play from that point.

The defensive team returns to its goal line on each play, and the offensive team repeats the same procedure. If no touchdown is scored in four tries, the defense becomes the offense and gets the ball at its twenty-yard line. Both teams must walk while the ball is in play. If the defense breaks its chain, it must reunite before proceeding down the field. If the offensive chain breaks, the down is automatically over. Score the game using any point system you wish.

Fris Ball

This game is played like softball, with the following adaptations:
■ Any number of players can play.
■ A Frisbee is used instead of a bat and a ball.
■ Each team gets six outs instead of three.
■ The Frisbee must go at least thirty feet on a fly or it is foul.
■ The offensive team does not have to wait until the defensive team is ready before sending their batter to the plate. This keeps to a minimum the normal slowdown between innings.

Kooky Kick Ball

This game can be played on either a baseball diamond or an open field. Like regular kick ball (or baseball), one team is at bat and the other is in the field.

The first player kicks the ball as it is rolled to her or him by a teammate. A miss, a foul, or a ball caught in the air is an out. Each team is allowed three outs per inning. If no outs are made, the inning ends after everyone on the team has been "at bat" once. When the ball is kicked, a fielder retrieves the ball and the rest of the fielding team lines up behind her or him. The ball is passed back between the legs of all the players. The last team member in line takes the ball and tries to tag the runner.

After kicking the ball, the kicker does not run around the bases. Instead, her or his team lines up single file behind the kicker, who runs around her or his team as many times as possible. One run is scored for every complete revolution the kicker makes before she or he is tagged.

Lap Sit

This cooperative game requires that everyone do a part, or the game flops. It is best with large groups, from fifty to five hundred and even more.

Have the group form a large circle with everyone facing one direction—clockwise or counterclockwise. Make sure the spacing between each player is about the same. Usually about twelve to eighteen inches is ideal. At a signal, have the players hold their arms out to the sides and sit down in the lap of the person immediately behind them. The trick is to have everyone hold everyone else up, but if one person is out of place, the whole group will most likely fall down.

The fun of this game is trying to succeed on the first try. If the players are not successful, have them try again until they finally succeed. After they have succeeded, have the group walk while in the seated position. This *really* takes coordination on everyone's part.

Plunger Ball

Young people enjoy this variation of baseball. This game can be played indoors or outdoors. You need a large rubber or plastic ball and a toilet plunger.

Divide the group into two teams. Pick one team to go to the field and the other to bat. The player at bat pokes at the ball with the rubber end of the plunger and runs to first base, and so on. All the normal rules of baseball or softball apply.

Change the rules as you see fit. For example, it is usually best to have four or five bases positioned close together. Boundaries and positions can be adjusted spontaneously. Players can be called out by hitting them with the ball. You can have five outs per inning.

Tube Mania

This exhausting game can be lots of fun.

Mark a large square in the field and place a stack of seven to ten inner tubes in the center of the square. Divide the group into four equal teams. Have one team line up on each side of the square and number the players on each team.

The object of the game is for each team to get as many inner tubes as possible across its own line. Call one, two, three, or four numbers. The players with those numbers run to the center and start dragging the inner tubes to their line. The number or numbers called will determine the number of players tugging on the same tube. Each tube successfully pulled across a team's line scores a point for that team.

Once the players get the hang of it, add a soccer ball to the game. Each team gets a point deducted from the score if the ball is kicked over its line. Team members along the line act as goalies. Each time the ball touches the ground in a team's territory, a point is deducted.

To further complicate the game, add a cage ball (four to eight feet in diameter). The team that gets this ball across their own line gets three points. The team with the most points wins.

Tug-of-War Times Two

Divide the group into four teams for a four-way tug-of-war. Tie two ropes together in the middle so that you have four equal lengths. Draw a circle on the ground. Put the knot at dead center and have each team pick up its rope and stand outside the circle.

Explain that when one team is pulled across the circle boundary, it is eliminated. Then the three remaining teams play until another team is eliminated. Finally, two teams play to determine the winner.

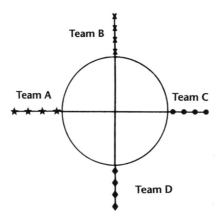

For Tug-of-War Times Three, tie together three ropes and begin with six teams. It works! The primary advantage to this version is that the lighter or weaker teams can gang up on the heavier or stronger teams and eliminate them from the game early on.

Nine-Legged Race

Just for fun or to demonstrate the value of working together, play this variation of the three-legged race. It works best with large groups, and it requires lots of space. You will need a supply of sacks or ropes or belts to join teammates together.

Divide the players into equal-size groups. (For this explanation, groups of eight are used.) Place five players from each team on one side of the field. Each team's remaining three players must stand opposite their teammates, across the field. From the five-player side, have two people from each team begin a traditional three-legged race. (Caution the players that even though you may not have called the game a *foot* race, the teammates cannot drop to their knees and pull themselves along with their hands.) When they reach the other side, have them add another team member, turn, and run back. At each end of their course they are to tie up with another teammate until all eight players are strung together at the ankles and running the last length. The first team across the finish line wins. (The *real* fun is watching the teams figure out how to turn around—but do not tell them this.)

For heightened hilarity, use thin strips of plastic trash bags as ties and add this rule—if a tie breaks, the team has to stop and either retie it or replace it.

Two-Base Ball

This is one of the all-time great games for large groups. It is exciting and lots of fun to play. It is best to have teams of about twenty to twenty-five playing on a big open field.

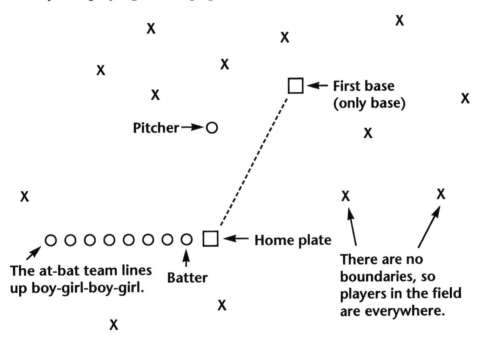

Use only two bases—home plate and first base (place first base about one hundred feet from home plate). Play with a regular baseball or softball bat and a volleyball with some of the air let out. Explain these rules to the teams:

There are no out-of-bounds and no foul balls. The ball can be hit in any direction. In fact, when the ball is pitched, the batter can attempt to hit it behind her or him.

The team at bat lines up boy-girl-boy-girl on one side of home plate.

The only field positions are a catcher and a first-base player and general outfielders. The team at bat provides its own pitcher. The pitch should be as easy to hit as possible. If the bat touches the ball in any way, it is a fair ball. Outs are made in the following ways:

- a missed swing (a strike is an out)
- a fly ball that is caught (as in regular baseball)
- a force-out at first base (as in regular baseball)
- a runner is tagged with the ball (the runner can be hit with the ball while running to or from first base)

Once a runner reaches first base, he or she does not have to leave until it is safe to do so, even if the next batter gets a hit. Any number of players can occupy first base at the same time. No runs are scored, however, until players cross home plate. For example, several players on first base might all run to home plate at the same time and score several runs.

Each team gets three outs per inning. As soon as the team at bat has three outs, those players run out into the field. The team at bat quickly lines up and starts hitting. It does not have to wait for the fielding team to get ready.

If you have more than fifty players, get two games going at once on opposite sides of the field. Let the games overlap. It can get very confusing, but it is a lot of fun. Each game will need an umpire to keep score and rule on controversial plays.

Long Jump Relay

Divide the contestants into teams of six or eight people, mark a starting line, and have each team form a single-file line behind it.

This is how the game works: At a signal, the first person in each line does a standing broad jump straight ahead—both feet must leave the ground simultaneously. The next player in line runs to him or her, places his or her feet exactly where the first jumper's feet were, and does another standing broad jump. The third player runs up to the second and repeats the process. Each player in turn rushes forward and jumps from where the preceding player landed.

After the last player of every team has jumped, the total distance of each team is measured. The team with the farthest distance wins.

Ultimate Frisbee Football

This variation on football has a twist that is guaranteed to tire even the most rambunctious players. It lets everyone play quarterback and receiver. The only equipment that you will need is a Frisbee.

Play on a football-type field with goal lines at either end. Explain that the object is to cross the opponent's goal line with the Frisbee. Play relies on passing the Frisbee to move it downfield.

If the Frisbee holder does not throw it by the time an opponent counts to ten, the Frisbee holder must run with the Frisbee and can be legally tagged by an opposing team member. The Frisbee changes teams in the case of a tag, an interception, or an incomplete pass.

Broom Hockey

This variation on hockey can be played with as many as thirty or as few as five people per team. However, only five or six members from each team are allowed on the field at one time. If you have a team of thirty members, have them number off by sixes, creating six sub-teams of five members each. Let all the 1s play a three-minute period, then the 2s, and so on.

In the center of the playing field, place a volleyball. And in front of each goal, line up brooms for the players (see diagram). At the sound of a whistle, the two teams should run onto the field, grab their brooms, and try to swat the volleyball through the opposing team's goal. Goalies can put the ball back into play by throwing it onto the playing field. If the ball goes out-of-bounds, a referee must throw it back in. While the ball is in play, it cannot be touched with hands or feet, only with brooms. Score one point each time the ball passes between goal markers or into the net.

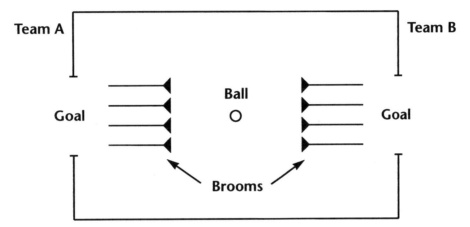

Sponge Dodge

In the heat of the summer, find a beach (or an open lawn with a garden hose handy), take along a half-dozen five-gallon buckets and an equal number of sponges, and play this game to cool off.

Mark out a circle and place the buckets around the perimeter. Half fill them with water and drop a sponge in each. After the entire youth group gets in the circle, soak the first sponge and throw it at someone. That person can join you around the edge of the circle and begin throwing sponges, too. Continue the game until only one person is left inside the circle—he or she is the winner. Sponges that drop inside the circle can be retrieved by any thrower, but they must be dipped again before they are thrown.

Some variations:
■ Play a couple rounds by teams. Time how long it takes for one team to eliminate members of an opposing team. The team that does so in the shortest time wins. Or set a time limit and declare the winner to be the team with the most members in the circle when the clock runs out.
■ Let the game run indefinitely, with no winners or losers. Begin the game with five inside the circle. Whoever makes a hit trades places with his or her victim.

Outdoor Games for Small Groups

All the games in this section are ideal for groups of thirty or fewer people in an outdoor setting. These games can also be played with larger groups, often with little or no adaptation.

Frisbee Soccer

For this variation on soccer, use a Frisbee instead of a soccer ball. All other rules of soccer apply. Soccer cages should be used so that they stop the Frisbee when the goal is made. You could also use a hoop or a tire that the Frisbee must pass through to score a goal. Players must move the Frisbee by tossing it from one player to another. They cannot run with the Frisbee.

Another version of this game is to have a Frisbee free-for-all between two teams. A dozen or two dozen Frisbees are placed in the center of the playing area. When the game starts, players try to get as many Frisbees as possible into their opponent's goal. Once a Frisbee is in a net, it stays there. Again, the Frisbees may only be passed. This is really a wild game.

Inner Tube Soccer

This is a game of soccer that follows the usual rules of the game, but it substitutes an inner tube (the size and shape of an automobile-tire tube) for the soccer ball. The tube should lie on the ground (like a hockey puck), and the playing surface should be relatively flat and smooth.

Circle Soccer

Play this variation of soccer with a soccer ball and on a soccer field. Divide the group into two teams. Select two people, one from each team, to be roaming players and have them stand opposite each other on either side of the center line. Have each team form a half-circle around its roamer so that together the two teams make a circle (see diagram). Explain that the object of the game is to kick the soccer ball through the other team's half of the circle. Hands may not be used at all, only feet and bodies. If the ball is kicked over the heads of the players, the point goes to the opposing team. No one may move out of position except the roaming players, who may kick the ball to their teammates if the ball stops in the center. The roaming players may not score points or cross into the other team's territory. If the roaming player gets hit with the ball when it is kicked by the opposing team, the kicking team gets a point.

When everyone is in place and ready, throw the ball into the circle and let the game begin!

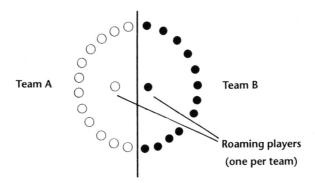

Roller Basketball

Using an outdoor basketball court, two teams on roller skates or roller blades attempt to score points by hitting the opponent's backboard with a beach ball. Teams can have five to ten players each. Players may either carry the ball or tap it, like in volleyball. If a player is tagged by an opponent while carrying the ball, the ball goes to the other team. The ball is then put in play by a player from the possessing team who passes it from out-of-bounds. A roughness penalty (use basketball rules) gives the opposing team a free throw from the free throw line.

Duck Ball

This game is kick ball with a twist. (Impose a one-pitch per kicker limit if the group is large.) Before the kickers run to first base, they are handed a fully inflated balloon that they must keep between their knees as they run. The fielders, meanwhile, are also equipped with balloons between their knees. The pitchers are exempt, but are not allowed to assist their team at all. Fielders must waddle as best they can to retrieve the ball and attempt to put the runners out. Outs are made by touching runners with the ball, either by a tag or a throw. Balls thrown out-of-bounds limit a runner to a single base.

Points are scored by crossing home plate—but that is not the only way. If a fielder pops his or her balloon, the other team scores a point. Likewise, if a runner pops his or her balloon, the fielding team scores a point. The game ends when a team earns twenty points or when a predetermined number of innings have been played.

You will need about fifty or sixty balloons in a large plastic bag or trash can to begin the game, and perhaps more as the game progresses. Those who do not want to play or cannot play can be recruited to maintain the balloon supply and to hand balloons to runners on their way to first base.

For indoor games, use a Nerf ball rather than a kick ball.

Jungle Football

This is essentially touch or flag football. However, all players are eligible to catch a pass. The quarterback (ball carrier) is permitted to run across the line of scrimmage and to pass the ball in any direction—forward, backward, and so on—to another player. Multiple passes are allowed. Each team gets four downs to score. There are no first downs. Only touchdowns (six points) and safeties (two points) are counted. The rules can be changed or modified to fit any size group, any age, and so on. Have your own Jungle Football Super Bowl!

Jump or Dive

This old camp favorite requires midair decision-making. You will need a swimming pool with a diving board. This is how it works: One at a time the young people take a nice, high bounce off the diving board. At the height of their jump, the leader yells either "Jump!" or "Dive!" and the young people must obey. Their execution is ruled a dive if a hand hits the water first, a jump if a foot hits first.

If the young people get too good at second-guessing the leader, he or she may choose to wait longer before yelling commands. Or he or she may really tie the players in knots with an occasional command to "Jive!"

Field Handball

For this hybrid of football and soccer, you will need a large ball (soccer ball, football, volleyball—even a kick ball will do), two durable chairs, and tape or rope. Pylons to mark the field boundaries and armbands to distinguish teams are optional.

Mark off a goal circle at each end of the field. The circles should be twelve feet in diameter. Put a chair in the middle of each one. The goal of the game is simply to hit the opponent's chair with the ball.

The game is played this way:

■ Start with a face-off in the center circle.
■ Players may run with the ball or pass the ball to a teammate.
■ If a runner is tagged, she or he has three seconds to pass the ball to a teammate. If the runner fails to pass the ball, the other team takes possession on the spot.

- If a player drops a pass from a teammate, anyone can pick up the ball and continue play.
- An intercepted pass is played without a break.
- No one, defender or attacker, may enter either of the goal circles. If this happens, the ball changes possession and play is renewed at the nearest boundary line.
- Following a goal, play begins again in center field.

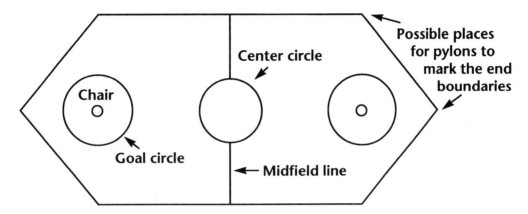

Soakin' Summer Softball

Make your softball (or whiffle ball or kick ball) games into summer cool-offs with these wet versions.

- Lay a Slip 'n' Slide or something similar between third base and home plate. Require runners to literally slide home all the way from third base.
- Substitute a lawn sprinkler for the bag at first base. Runners who hit a modest single must straddle the sprinkler. The more fortunate, who hit at least a double, have only to jump over the sprinkler on their way to second. A base runner on first and a pitcher with a slow windup equals one sopping player!

To keep both games moving, limit the batter to one pitch—either a hit or an out.

Fizzer Tag

Before you play this summertime game, drill a small hole in the center of as many Alka Seltzer tablets as you have players and run a separate long piece of string through each tablet. Have the players tie their tablet loosely around their neck. Supply each person with a squirt gun (or in advance tell the players to bring one). Establish boundaries and place several buckets of water out-of-bounds for filling and refilling the squirt guns.

Now begin a game of Fizzer Tag. When a player's Alka Seltzer tablet gets hit enough and dissolves sufficiently to drop off the string, that player is out. To shorten the game, bring out the garden hose!

Kick Golf

No green fees are needed for this round of golf! Set up your own nine-hole course: Hula Hoops become "greens," small sticks stuck within them become "flags," and small playground balls become "golf balls." A leg and foot make a "golf club." Lay markers of some sort to show where players tee off. And do not forget to set par: use hills and other "traps" to vary the difficulty of each "hole." When the ball touches the stick, it is considered to be in the hole.

Distribute score cards and play by teams if you like.

Wolleyball

This game is great for a group with people of varying ages or skill levels. It suits younger players who may not yet be well-coordinated and is challenging to the more athletic people. Lower the volleyball net until the bottom edge touches the floor or play on a tennis court. Use a kick ball. The game is like traditional volleyball in most ways:

- The six-person team rotates.
- Only the serving team can score.
- The teams are allowed a maximum of three hits per volley.
- No two consecutive hits by any one player are allowed.
  Here are the differences:
- Servers serve as in two-square—they bounce the ball once, then hit it over the net.
- Teammates can help a lagging serve over the net.
- The ball may bounce once (but does not have to) before a team returns it, as well as between the two or three hits a team makes before returning the ball over the net.

Guru

The gurus in your group will love this hide-and-seek game. It is perfect for summer evenings. Select one of the young people to be the guru, who is to dress in an identifying robe. Give the guru a lit candle and have him or her hide somewhere within the boundaries of the game. When the guru is settled, direct the other players, each armed with a squirt gun and an unlit candle, to spread out to find the guru.

As players discover the guru, they are to light their own candle from his or hers and, by stealth more than speed, try to get back to a designated home base before their candle is extinguished by others' squirt guns. Emphasize that the guru's candle cannot be extinguished by other players. If their flame gets doused, the players must return to the guru to relight their candle. The first player to arrive at home base with a lit candle is the winner.

Caution the players that if their candle gets squirted out and they have to return to the guru for a light, they should not expect to find him or her in the same place—for the guru can move around at will.

Inner Tube Open

This game can be won by sheer inexperience—so look out, golf pros! You will need one or two nine-iron golf clubs, a dozen tennis balls (six yellow, six orange), a large blanket (or tarp), and a large, inflated inner tube.

Spread out the blanket and mark a line ten to twelve feet away from the front edge of it. Have the players putt from behind this line. Place the inner tube on the far edge of the blanket (see diagram). Players get six strokes to earn points in the following ways:
- one point if the ball hits the blanket
- three points if the ball stays on the blanket
- five points if the ball hits the inner tube
- twenty points if the ball lands inside the inner tube

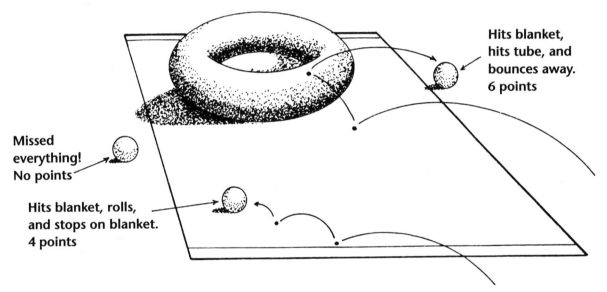

Hits blanket, hits tube, and bounces away. 6 points

Missed everything! No points

Hits blanket, rolls, and stops on blanket. 4 points

Here is what makes this game fun: Points are awarded cumulatively. That is, if a ball hits the inner tube (five points), rolls across the blanket a ways (one point), and remains on the blanket (three points), the player earns nine points. Or if a ball hits the inner tube but bounces away without touching the blanket, that player earns five points. The player with the most points wins. This game can be played by teams or by individuals.

Run 'n' Wet

Got your swimsuits on? Have the players sit in a circle and number off. Then put a plump water balloon in the center of the circle. When you call out two numbers, the two whose number is called must jump up and run around the circle and back to their own place. Then they must race to the water balloon in the middle. Can you guess the rest? The first one there gets to throw the balloon at the loser, who must stand still and not dodge it.

Taxi

This swimming-pool game begins with two teams on opposite sides of the pool. Give each team an air mattress. On the signal "go," one member of each team should straddle the mattress and paddle it around the pool. When the players arrive back at their own starting point, they must each pick up another teammate and make another lap. This continues until the entire team is on the mattress.

The trick is mounting the mattress, especially with several people already on it. There will be a lot of thrashing and sputtering during this game!

Midnight Volleyball

Start a volleyball game shortly before dark. Play by the customary rules *until* the genuine question, "Where is it?" is shouted by someone—at this point the game changes to Midnight Volleyball.

- The game ends when a team makes five points. A team can win by one point, rather than the customary two-point spread.
- A team can hit the ball as many times as it needs to, provided the ball does not touch the ground.

Play the best two out of three games—if you can stand it that long and if parents allow their children to stay out that late. This game is a blend of frustration, challenge, and a lot of fun mixed with blind luck instead of skill.